ZINGERS!

ZINGERS!

A New Approach to Getting a Job, Changing Careers & Getting Ahead

Joanna Henderson
Betty Lou Marple

amacom

AMERICAN MANAGEMENT ASSOCIATION

This book is available at a special
discount when ordered in bulk quantities.
For information, contact Special Sales Department,
AMACOM, a division of American Management Association,
135 West 50th Street, New York, NY 10020.

Library of Congress Cataloging-in-Publication Data

Henderson, Joanna
    Zingers! : a new approach to getting a job, changing careers, & getting ahead.

    Includes index.
    1. Success in business. I. Marple, Betty Lou.
II. Title
HF5386.H427   1988   650.1   87-47852
ISBN 0-8144-7696-1

Printing number

10 9 8 7 6 5 4 3 2 1

For
Heidi, Jennifer, and Peter

For
Caroline, Ted, and Doug

Acknowledgments

We thank all those who told us their own zingers or the zingers they knew of, and the countless others whose stories have become memorable zingers. We used as many as we could and wish we could have used them all in this book. We thank our agent, Mike Snell, for pushing us to get it right and for encouraging us along the way. We thank Nancy Brandwein, an editor who enjoyed the book as much as we did. Finally, we thank the two who stood behind us with moral and technical support, Skip and Wes.

Contents

Chapter 1

Lightning Bolts and Thunderclaps:
Grabbing Attention in a Competitive World

The clock on the wall said 6:30, well past the time that Carlton and Laird's selection committee had agreed to spend on reviewing candidates. Stacks of unsolicited resumes were piled on the oval oak conference table. Four people sat there: the director of recruiting, two division heads, and the audit manager, all of whom worked for a West Coast accounting firm. No one on that committee knew any of the applicants personally.

The past year had been a good one for Carlton and Laird, and anticipated growth meant there would be a healthy crop of new hires. Although not a Big Eight firm, C&L was large enough to hire 20 new trainees from the ranks of current college graduates. Now after three hours decisions about whom to invite for initial interviews had been made for all of the slots except one. The choice was between two women aspirants, both with excellent grades, great extracurricular activities, and the right course work for an accounting firm. Stomachs growled, spouses waiting elsewhere tapped their heels, and children watched yet one more round of TV shows while the four agonized.

"Let's come back to this tomorrow," groaned Fred, the audit manager. "No way. I have no time tomorrow and I couldn't face it again anyway," retorted Janet, the division head from the tax department. "This is the last one. Let's read both resumes over carefully, have everyone say one final statement about each candidate, and then vote." Ellen, who headed the electronic data processing services, was already reaching for the wall phone behind her. "Well, let me call my husband and add 15 minutes to pick-up time," she said, conceding.

While Ellen dialed, the rest of the group dug in for the final read-through. A few minutes later, Janet, who chaired the meeting, called for the review.

"John, go first," said Janet, her eyes on the clock.

"They're both so good," said John, the recruiting manager. "So similar too. But Marie Delisle did something really unusual with her computer skills. I'm talking about the program she wrote for that mail-order business. She's a real entrepreneur."

"It's funny you noticed that, because I had the same impression," said Fred, sitting up in his chair. "Now that we're looking at only these two resumes and not at 100 others, I see things I had missed on the first pass. Marie took her knowledge of a computer language a step further and did something really creative with it.''

Ellen had just gotten off the phone and was still reading, so Janet continued. ''Hmm. Here I was thinking I'd have a fight on my hands with you guys, because Kate Haskell got such high marks on the first round, but we see eye-to-eye on this. I'm in no position to evaluate mail-order software, and there probably isn't anyone in this company who is, but she's a hustler all right.''

Ellen looked up from reading just as Janet finished her endorsement of Marie Delisle. ''I didn't hear all of what you two said,'' she noted, looking at Fred and John, ''but I did hear Janet. I can't believe we ever saw these two as equally good candidates for the job. Sure, they look similar on paper at first, but once you see what Marie did with her ability to program, Kate pales. The funny thing is, it looks like she knows only one language, and it's an easy one to boot. The program she wrote probably isn't terribly sophisticated, but so what? She did something creative here. She's got ideas and drive, and I like her.''

The vote was taken, and the four filed out of the conference room, congratulating each other on such a quick finish as they headed for their offices and then out into the parking lot.

Janet had agreed to give John a ride to the subway station if they ran late, so both climbed into her black hatchback and took off, honking at the other two as they were waved through the security gate.

''You know what always amazes me,'' said John as he rummaged through pockets looking for subway change. ''So many decisions have to be made quickly without all the facts available, by people who are tired, grumpy, or bored, and it's almost always one thing that jumps off the resume or application or contract. That one thing is often not a huge achievement like outstanding grades or scores, or where the person works or went to school, but something kind of neat that just excites you. Look at what happened back there. We had two people with similar skills, talents, course work, extracurricular activities—the works. But Marie Delisle beat out Kate Haskell by a four-to-nothing vote because she held our attention when we read about the program she created for a business. It made her look like a real go-getter.''

Janet nodded and then began to smile. "I know exactly what you mean. I did something similar to that. When I was applying to graduate schools ten years ago, I wrote at length on my applications about the weekly radio show I'd done as an undergraduate. Dozens of students work at their college stations, but I'd created a talk show that had a big listening audience because I would pit against each other two people who disagreed over a local issue. Then I gave them air time and let it fly.

"In all my interviews we ended up talking about that radio show. It jumped off the application every time, and once I started talking about it, the conversation never got back to anything else. I think I got into so many graduate schools because of that—what? What do you call it when something on the printed page or in conversation just grabs you and you want to know more? It's always something that seems ordinary, but goes a step or two further, the sort of thing anybody could do."

John laughed. "I don't know what you call it, but I see examples all the time. Your story and Marie Delisle's remind me of Chris Monroe down in the legal department. He told me how he got his title changed. He has been pushing his boss for a change for months, not only because his title doesn't reflect what he really does now but because he has saved the company a ton of money this year in fending off legal attacks."

Janet looked confused. "How is a title change like a job interview?"

"It's the method he used. He wrote a proposal for the title change listing all the logical reasons he should be a vice president and then included an update on his recent activities, including the fact that he is writing a series of articles for his local paper. These have nothing to do with Carlton and Laird. They are just arm-chair lawyering articles about taxes and mortgages, but they're good stuff, and they put C&L's name next to a nice series for a few weeks. His boss was so impressed that apparently all the logical reasons why he should be a VP washed right over as he focused on the free public relations piece, and darned if Chris didn't get the new title a couple of weeks later. Here's the killer though. He's not telling many people, but the whole idea came to him through a classified ad he wrote."

"Classified ad for what?" Janet asked. "I don't get the connection."

"The classified was for his social life," John explained. "Haven't you been reading about how single people are finding each other through the classifieds?"

"No," said Janet, "and here's your subway stop, but don't get out until I hear this one."

"Well, he wrote an ad, just a brief but very classy 20 words or so designed to attract the type of woman he was interested in—well-educated and upscale but also sensitive, giving, and the rest. In addition to describing himself as the male version of all those adjectives, he also inserted the words 'expert on sex discrimination cases,' without saying he was a lawyer. He did it because he thought that line would attract someone interesting who was curious about how he got to be an expert on an issue with which most men aren't involved." John paused for effect. "He's now dating another lawyer who has also handled sex discrimination cases and who responded to the ad. His words spoke to her. That ad turned out to be a real zinger."

"There you go. You found a name for what we were talking about—*zingers!*" Janet said, snapping her fingers.

John pulled his briefcase and raincoat from the back seat of the car. "See you tomorrow," he grinned, then he waved as he walked toward the subway.

WHAT THOSE ZINGERS CAN DO

Zingers! Everyone has the potential for creating them in all kinds of life circumstances—to get an edge on the competition for a promotion, a contract, a job in a crowded market, attention, a better social life, admission to college—whenever standing out in a positive way can determine success.

The dictionary says that a zinger can be "something causing or meant to cause interest, surprise, or shock." Zingers are important because throughout life there are endless situations when you have to compete for and attract someone's attention in order to reach your goals. When starting a business of your own, you must convince a banker, lawyer, accountant, venture capitalist, or friends and family that what you are trying to do is important and will work. How does an employer decide among so many people, almost all of whom could do the job well? How does a college admissions person select from among equally good applicants? And how does the banker or even a relative decide to loan you money unless you stand above the rest?

Decision makers rarely have the time, resources, and skills to dig into each candidate's history adequately, to siphon out those whose personal styles would best fit a particular group. Indeed, it is even illegal for an interviewer to probe into some of these areas. In any fiercely competitive market, zingers provide a quick way for people to distinguish themselves. Zingers are not just for show. They are not jazzy one-liners to slip into a resume or application for glitter. A zinger requires active performance. Ordinary people can be coached on finding methods for carrying out zingers and then writing them up in ways that will grab the reader's or listener's attention, as Marie Delisle did.

Just a Face in the Crowd

Let's backtrack to a time before the Carlton and Laird staff convened around their oak table and put both Kate Haskell and Marie Delisle under a microscope. Kate was a business major who had indeed worked hard. Her grades from a state university in northern California made teachers and parents proud. Her extracurricular activities were numerous and included a range from sports and music to computers. She was ambitious and had always held part-time jobs in the library and the school cafeteria. She knew a computer language well, and had traveled abroad twice, once to Switzerland with her family and another time to Scotland with a group of friends.

But Kate did not do well in her job search. As a senior, she interviewed selectively but actively for three months and received no offers. The letters of rejection were polite, perhaps even a bit too elaborate in their discussion of why she was not wanted, but they were all clear in their final message. She was told that she was good, she was bright, she had worked hard, but she was not special enough for the firms where she had interviewed. What is wrong here? Why did Kate have such difficulty landing her first job? Some years ago, she would have been sitting on top of half a dozen job offers by spring of her senior year and would be agonizing over which offer to accept.

Two important changes have come about in recent years. First, we have come to expect college graduates to have done most of the things Kate has. Her accomplishments sound routine; she does not stand out in any way. Indeed, she is quite ordinary in a work world full of well-rounded graduates. That leads us to the second change, the sheer number of people with whom Kate is competing for attention. Not only are there over a million college graduates annually now, there are in addition thousands more who hold MBAs and other specialized graduate degrees—a dizzying number of bright-enough, achievement-oriented young people, all of whom have held good summer jobs or internships, traveled, learned about computers, and been given solid advice from their career planning and placement offices, in addition to reading all the books on preparing resumes and interviewing well.

Kate, a bright plodder, took advantage of available opportunities, yet she did not aggressively seek ways to stand out from her peers. There was not a zinger on her resume, nor was there one in her history. Through no fault of her own, she did not learn to create zingers.

Getting Noticed

Marie Delisle had the same major as Kate and had similar job experiences. Although she had not traveled as much as Kate had, she held the post of treasurer of the University Marching Band at her school in North Carolina, a 15-hour-a-week paid job, in addition to playing in the band. Her computer skills were good, although not brilliant. She knew one language well and could manipulate two or three statistical packages. Nothing zingy so far. But Marie knew she needed to set herself apart if she wanted interviewers to pay attention, and she had learned from her father how to look at every opportunity with an eye to taking it further, making more out of routine experiences. Occasionally they fizzled, but she always learned something, and this propelled her on to the next idea, which might evolve as a zinger.

Marie believed that having learned a computer language, she could write a small program that could be used by someone to perform a simple function. Then she would have a nice accomplishment to add to her resume, one that would give her an edge over students who knew a computer language but had never written programs that were actually used. She understood that it was the use of a program by someone who needed it—whose time would be saved, whose work load would be lightened, and whose gratitude would be obvious—that would be critical here. She began to look for an opportunity to write a relatively simple computer program.

As band treasurer she was well aware that the band's financial activities were neither well documented nor accessible. There seemed to be little information about how money deposited from fund-raising events was used. There was no hint of fraud, simply poor record keeping. Marie enlisted the help of her computer sciences professor and the band director and set out to write a program that would track money generated from fund-raising events. It was an unsophisticated program, but it performed the necessary functions. Marie, pleased with the results from her first usable program, decided to tackle a more difficult programming chore. Her mother, who ran a mail-order business from the family home in Salem, North Carolina, did her own accounting using an antiquated handwritten ledger. Marie thought she could use the band's program as the core of a program for her mother's business, but that did not work and she realized that an entirely new program was needed. The results after debugging were good. Once Marie's mother was shown how to use the new program, she was pleased. Her books were more accurate and she had more time to spend on promotion and sales.

Marie then wrote up her successes as a computer programmer and had two zingers. This is how they appeared on her resume.

WORK EXPERIENCE: Free-lance Computer Programmer

Wrote computer program for North Carolina State University Music Department to track financial information from fund-raising events. Program has been in use for four years. Documentation available.

Wrote computer program for The Hobbyist, a mail-order business located in Salem, North Carolina, netting $170,000 in annual revenues. Analyzed accounting problems of business, worked closely with owner to design, write, and debug program, which saves owner 20 hours of labor weekly. Documentation available.

With these entries on her resume, Marie presents a picture of a talented and imaginative young woman. Not only are we aware of specific technical skills, but we see a product, one that may even have a commercial market. Marie has made us pay attention. Should Marie decide to go on and market her program to other small mail-order firms, she could add even more panache to her write-up. Imagine her resume thus:

WORK EXPERIENCE: Entrepreneur

Designer of SOFTMAIL, a computer program used by mail-order houses to track and manage financial information used in this industry. Have successfully marketed and sold SOFT-MAIL to three mail-order companies. Developing strategy for national advertising.

In order to develop SOFTMAIL, Marie would probably have to collaborate with a friend or two whose programming skills are more sophisticated. Even if Marie's idea to advertise nationally never takes off, or if the other two customers are business colleagues of her mother's, the achievement is a zinger. It is important to focus on the overall achievement, to write it up surrounded by justifiably positive aspects. Then, one can speak about it with vigor.

Kate Haskell could have developed a similar zinger, perhaps even a better one. She was as bright, skilled, and hard working as Marie Delisle. Since she had travel experiences which Marie lacked, she could have viewed those as opportunities to create zingers. Perhaps she could have made a short video on Swiss chocolate factories or interviewed Scots in local pubs to get their reaction to North Sea oil drilling, which had brought employment but had altered the character of many small Scottish towns.

Unfortunately, Kate has been taught that all she needs to do to set her apart is write a thank you note to a recruiter after the interview and enclose a copy of an article about a subject the two discussed. A few years ago that might have worked, but today most people write thank you's and often clippings are enclosed. This once-effective tactic has now become a cliché. The real beauty of a true zinger is its uniqueness; no two are the same.

Playing the Match Game—and Winning

Obviously, a zinger used for getting into the college of your choice is not going to work for moving up to the next rung on the corporate ladder. Nor will an effective corporate zinger work if you are a 40-year-old woman whose last child has just gone off to college and are looking for your first job, or if you're an executive who's just been handed early retirement and who wants to get a bank loan in order to start your own business. There are levels of appropriateness for zingers depending on how they will be viewed by the person on the decision-making side of the table. Also, there are zingers that relate in some way to the prize being sought, be it admission to a school, the granting of a contract, or acceptance by an association. Other zingers that are in no way related to the prize may be equally effective. Included in the following chapters are both simple and sophisticated zingers to use in widely diverse situations and by a range of age groups.

Job-Related Zingers

If we take another look at the case of Chris Monroe who works in the legal department of Carlton and Laird, we see a zinger that is related directly to Chris's work. Months before he actually wrote the list of reasons why he should be made a vice president, it was clear to the Philadelphia lawyer that, even within a legal department, logic and reason would not prevail and would play only a marginal part in the decision about his title change. As well intentioned as we all mean to be, it is human nature to decide largely in favor of people we like, whether the occasion is to invite them for dinner, give them a raise, or recommend them for admission to our alma mater.

Chris was at a disadvantage because he was bucking the rules at C&L, which state that only two people in any department may hold the title of vice president, and because he was competing against another person also hoping for the VP title. Further, his boss was only marginally interested in the problem of a title change for Chris. The two knew each other superficially because they worked in different cities. Chris's task was first to raise his hand and be noticed, and then to get the person whose attention he sought to like him. Both of these were accomplished with a zinger.

Chris planned ahead and decided that a six-part series in his suburban newspaper on topical legal issues would be a bonus. It was not difficult to persuade a local paper to let him write the series once he contacted the appropriate person, outlined his plan, and submitted a writing sample in the form of the first article for the series. Local newspapers are almost always eager for good, current copy related to a regional area of interest or written by a resident of the community.

The series ran, and Chris clipped not only the articles but also the letters to the editor from readers who responded positively (and in some cases even asked for the series to be extended). He submitted these clippings as an appendix to his title-change proposal.

Why did Chris's boss decide after reading the proposal that his subordinate was entitled to the upgrade? Chris showed creativity and leadership in his zinger, and these are the two critical elements in effective zingers. Both do not need to be present in every achievement, but the very definition of a zinger implies that one of these is apparent. People tend to like those who show creativity or leadership in any area, because they will probably demonstrate the same qualities in the new situation, whether at school, on the job, or in a social context.

Unrelated Zingers

At a high-tech company in Portland, Maine, an important employee representatives committee met to discuss outside consultants being considered for the task of conducting a study on low morale in the company. Seven or eight different companies had been approached for the job. None of the employees knew any of the people whose brochures and resumes were being passed around the table and discussed. Suddenly Bob O'Hara said, "Listen to this. Under Charles Austin's hobbies it says, 'hot-air balloon enthusiast, avid collector of antique balloons, and speaker on the subject. Have traveled over 100,000 miles in hot-air balloons. Currently planning group trip next summer of 80 balloons from New Jersey to Saskatchewan.' "

The group stopped reading to listen, and then someone said, "Hey, that's neat. What an interesting guy. He'd be fun to meet." Within minutes, the group voted to have the consulting firm of Charles L. Austin Associates come and interview. Charles Austin's zinger had made his company interesting, and when he came in to talk the employees were even more captivated by his unusual hobby. Early in the meeting it was established that Austin could do the job. The bulk of the interview was spent in asking him questions about his ballooning expertise. He was hired for the job and still stands out as an interesting person. This zinger had nothing to do with the job sought, but it worked.

Some will argue that this is no way to select a management consultant. Others would wonder why Bob O'Hara and his group did not carefully rank all of the competing consulting firms, assigning points for various services offered, references reviewed, credentials examined, schools attended, degrees conferred, satisfied customers accumulated, and more.

There are indeed a wide variety of analytical methods developed for choosing people for a specific job, but those techniques are not often used and usually do not work well when they are applied. Because most of us want to feel good about the decisions we make in selecting people, we usually make judgments based on what we intuitively sense is right rather than on how people rank on scales.

Also, we often do not have time to go through the mechanics of analytical ratings and procedures because a decision is called for quickly.

That is not to suggest that choosing people because of their
zingers always results in the best candidate receiving the nod (although this may be true), but that is the way people are hired or
chosen. Whether it is for better or for worse, we choose someone
because we like that person, and zingers often play a significant role
in our liking someone quickly.

Traditional Zingers

In more conservative professions, Charles Austin's hot-air ballooning might not have worked as effectively, but there are many
zingers that do the job of attracting attention through the demon-
stration of creativity or leadership in a less ostentatious way. Here
we find the university vice president in Denver who suggested, organized, and implemented the founding of the first pre-law advisers
organization in the country. She wrote up her experience this way
on her resume:

PAST ACCOMPLISHMENTS:

Suggested the idea, organized the committee, and helped im-
plement the founding of the first pre-law advisers organization
in the country. This culminated in a two-day conference at
Williams College attended by over 100 people. The organization is still active eight years later and holds an annual conference.

This is an achievement almost any academic person could have
conceived and organized, but our woman did it first.

There are endless firsts still out there because new problems,
populations, products, and services keep appearing, in the process
replacing outdated ones. This academic zinger may not appear as
catchy as some others, but in its subdued way, geared toward the
audience for which it was designed, it worked—it showed both creativity and leadership.

To Thine Own Self Be True

Zingers can be used to build confidence too. Sometimes we need achievements in our heads to give us the strength to tackle the next problem or project. It might not be included in a resume or proposal, nor discussed in an interview or even at a cocktail party. But it earns its reward by our knowing we did it and makes it possible for us to attack the next opportunity.

One clever Detroit woman spent several years working her way through the maze of problems in adopting an Asian baby. She decided to put together a directory of U. S. agencies that help couples do the same thing. Once her baby was safely in its cradle, she researched, wrote, and marketed her directory, finally getting it published by a small not-for-profit press. This zinger was never used in any move-ahead scheme, but the author suddenly had a new image of who she was. She realized she had untapped skills. She developed the confidence to take on something large because of the zinger in her head.

NON-ZINGERS

Not everything that gets attention is a zinger, even if it does show leadership or creativity. A zinger is not something that happens to you, but something that you make happen. Sitting in a restaurant at a table close to a local sports hero who starts a conversation with you is not a zinger. Going to school with the son of the Secretary of State or attending the Cannes Film Festival are not zingers. These are all relatively passive acts and simply don't constitute what we call a zinger, although each could be carried the next step and become a true zinger with a little creative thinking. The following exercise will help you to identify the best zinger for each situation and to recognize a non-zinger when you see one.

* * * *

Exercise: How Do You Know
When a Zinger Zings?

Part A. Problems

Select the answer you believe is the most appropriate.

1. Marian Heffernan has just moved to Cleveland to join a large law firm. At the first meeting she attends of a woman's legal networking group she is asked to introduce herself and say a few words about her work and what is important to her. She chooses to mention which one of the following?

   a. That she designed and built her own log vacation home.

   b. That she recently won $10,000 in a state lottery and plans to donate a substantial portion to the legal-aid society in Cleveland.

2. Andy DeNault has been invited to interview for a job in the market research department of a large West Coast electronics firm. He goes to the interview prepared to toss which of the following into the conversation?

   a. That he organized and taught a preschool class for three- to five-year-olds at his church.

   b. That he started a pushcart business on the main street in his home town selling brownies and freshly squeezed lemonade for three summers while in college and grossed a total of $9,000.

3. Nina Brinkley, a high school biology teacher in Oklahoma City, is writing a grant proposal to allow her students to set up a small-scale hydroponics project in order to study food production without soil. In the proposal she discusses at length which of these choices?

   a. That she produced a video on shore birds that has been used in elementary school science programs.

   b. That, as a volunteer project, she created the designs and wrote the text for all of the campaign literature used by her Republican congressman, who is up for election this year.

4. Leslie Halverson started her own business just eight months ago producing a financial newsletter for people in forest products industries. Her business has grown fast, and Leslie has run out of start-up money. She needs cash and credit fast. In preparing for an interview with her bank in Eugene, Oregon, she contemplates the following two choices to

highlight in her conversation. Which one makes the best zinger in this situation?

a. That she worked part time as a bank teller in college, and during an attempted robbery she kept her cool, let the police inside the bank before the holdup men could get away, and wrote up her angle of the story for publication in several newspapers.

b. That she won the Miss Junior New Jersey contest when she was in high school and traveled throughout the state one summer to promote the products of the cola company that had sponsored the contest.

5. One of the three assistant vice presidents in George Trickler's division of an interstate bank in Atlanta will soon be made senior treasurer. All three have excellent records and went through the same training program together. George plans to highlight his management and leadership skills by letting the committee know:

a. That he is the organizer and president of an anti-nuclear-power group in his county.

b. That he helped his community establish a transfer station to replace the former dump site, became an expert on transfer stations, and has spoken frequently on the subject.

6. Jeff Schumann has excellent grades and test scores that will no doubt impress many of the law schools to which he plans to apply. On several applications, he is asked to write an essay about a single outstanding experience from high school or college. Which of these two choices should he select for the essay?

a. That he did an internship in his Alaskan senator's Washington, D.C., office, where he helped research the best possible site for a new maximum-security prison in his state.

b. That he was co-founder and co-owner with his brother of Fast Lane Enterprises, a company that rented radar detectors, which they managed for three years.

Part B. Answers

1. Designing and building your own home, even if it is made from logs, is a significant achievement, so Marian ought to use this zinger (**a**) in her introduction. Winning the lottery, while it might indicate to some people that Marian is a lucky person, is still a passive act. Her number was simply drawn from a revolving drum. If you were swayed to choice

(b) by her largesse, think about the difference between creativity/leadership and generosity. The former demonstrates a skill, the latter is a wonderful personality trait. As a lawyer, Marian needs her new legal community to think of her as someone who is skilled not only professionally but in her personal life also. If they see her as generous, that is nice, but not critical.

But can you think of a way that Marian could have used the $10,000 to create a zinger?

2. The old rule about keeping religion and politics out of interviews and off the pages of applications holds true for zingers as well. Andy DeNault's Sunday school class (a) may have been brilliantly conceived and executed, but the mention of an organized religious group will turn off some people. It is not that he shouldn't become involved in these activities. But it's not a zinger because it could backfire eventually. The person on the other side of the interview table may not be able to separate the clear evidence of leadership from the basic religious commitment, which the interviewer may not share. Andy has a wonderful entrepreneurial achievement in his pushcart business (b) and he should use this one to the hilt. He will attract positive attention and be seen as a real hustler, a plus in any marketing position.

3. Nina Brinkley's choice is similar, but it is a bit more difficult because she has two good zingers. She could write up her accomplishment in designing the campaign literature (b) in a way that simply omits the mention of partisan politics. But her political activity should not really be used as the zinger because she will probably have to eventually identify the Republican to whom she gave so much support. If Nina's portfolio were thin, she might need to use this one, but why take the chance when she has a terrific zinger in her bird video (a)? It is unlikely that such an accomplishment will offend anyone, and it sounds like an interesting and valuable project. It immediately arouses interest. How is the video being used? Where did she do her shooting? Is it about all shore birds, or just those on the West Coast? If she produced a video that's currently in use in the classroom, she can probably set up a hydroponics project successfully.

4. Leslie's choice is a tricky one, because winning the beauty contest (b) allowed her to travel, act as a salesperson of sorts, and have a special opportunity not generally offered to high school students. Leslie can always throw in the beauty contest as a good learning experience, but handling the bank robbery (a) successfully is the zinger in this case for several reasons. It happened in a bank, the very environment Leslie will be entering to seek her loan. The banker's curiosity will be aroused

by the story and a rapport will be established. But, most important, she wrote the story up and got it published in the newspaper. She made the bank look good by leading readers to believe that the bank hires capable personnel. There may even be a halo effect, in which the loan officer will believe that she made one bank look good and she can make his bank look good too. It doesn't make sense in any logical way, but sometimes this works. Leslie could actually use both these achievements in an interview, highlighting the bank robbery but throwing in the beauty contest as an additional item in her portfolio.

5. Unless George Trickler is sure his boss is strongly anti-nuke, the transfer station project (**b**) is a better bet than the anti-nuclear project (**a**). It makes George look like a good citizen (which he is) and, better, yet, shows that he is an expert on a subject. Here is a guy who is not just sitting on a committee raising his hand to vote once in a while, but who has actually gotten involved with the subject. He has obviously read a lot, interviewed people, done some research, and knows his stuff. His boss and anyone else making the decision can hardly help but be impressed with the level of involvement in a community-based project.

6. Of course, if it were business school to which Jeff Schumann was applying, you would have chosen Fast Lane Enterprises (**b**) immediately as the zinger. But because Jeff is applying to law school, you may have felt the internship in a congressman's office (**a**) was more appropriate. Probably not. Doing a Washington internship, especially for a congressman, has become a cliché. So unless one works on an unusual project, one that is clearly different, this internship isn't even a zinger. Jeff may never have met the congressman, was surely one of several dozen students there at the same time in the same office, and did not appear to have done anything distinguishing. But Fast Lane Enterprises? Move over, this is a hot one. Whether Jeff wants a law school acceptance letter or a bank loan, a move up the corporate ladder or a blind date's approval, with this zinger he instantly demonstrates imagination, not to mention creativity and leadership. We want to hear more. Did he make money? (Some.) Who were his customers? (Mostly women.) Where is Fast Lane now? (Bought by a friend.) Did he make money on the sale of the company? (Yes.) This zinger takes the reader right down the garden path.

* * * *

By now you probably have a pretty good handle on what constitutes a zinger. The question now is how to cultivate your own and how to use them most effectively. The rest of this book is devoted to discussing different kinds of zingers and showing how they have been used by many different types of people, in a wide variety of situations, for diverse purposes. There are exercises in several chapters that allow you to work out a potential zinger on paper or in your head. The achievements in this book are all real and you will be able to create your own through the variety of examples presented.

Chapter 2

Small Is Beautiful:
Knowing More About Less

When Fred Miller, a lawyer in West Hamilton, Illinois, read in his local paper about the effects of acid rain in his state and county, he became alarmed and began to do some research on the topic. Fred read everything that had been written and then began to write his own commentary. He quickly became an expert on the subject and on what it meant for the area in which he lived. Soon he was asked to speak—first at places like the Kiwanis Club and then at a conference sponsored by environmentalists from five states who were forming a consortium to address the issue. Fred, who was happy enough working as a small-town lawyer, soon found himself propelled into the limelight because he had become an expert on an important topic of interest.

Fred's resume took on new interest with a section not on the *curriculum vitae* of most lawyers, and consequently it was a zinger for potential clients who wanted more than just a garden-variety attorney.

SPECIAL INTERESTS:

Knowledge of impact of acid rain on county and region; specialize in information on the chemical and political implications of changing the environment.

The consortium of environmental groups that sponsored the conference wanted to write a funding proposal to submit to a private foundation for a grant. Fred, as the official adviser to the group, wrote up his credentials in such a way as to persuade the foundation that he knew more than anyone about the subject. The consortium got its grant.

BECOME AN EXPERT

Becoming an expert is really easy. The trick is to pick a topic small enough to be mastered in a manageable time and then to relate the subject matter to your own home town, job, school, cause, or area. You may not become an expert instantly, but you can be one soon enough. Then you can go on to use this expertise publicly to further your own and others' agendas.

Meet some experts. They come from city and country, they are all ages, male and female. Each one, by doing what came naturally, took a personal concern and developed it into a larger activity, thereby achieving a greater goal.

Start first by meeting the most important expert: you. Think about all the things that have interested you. These may extend back to your childhood and may seem irrelevant until you think actively about them. Make a list of your interests and then think of the directions they may take you in. No one else need see this list, so dream of all the unfinished agendas you have and write them down. Then make a note of what you might like to do with them. Fred Miller's write-up may have been less dramatic than the final grant proposal, or it might have been even grander. The point is to get you thinking.

No matter how small or trivial your interest may be, you can be sure of two things: Someone else (maybe even hundreds or thousands of other people) will share your interest; that person (or people) would like to know more about it. It does not have to be about a life or death matter (although there are examples of people who have turned near catastrophes into zingers, including auto accidents and hospital visits). It does not need to involve many people or different kinds of people or people of different ages. The point is that your interest is genuinely *yours*.

A tragedy in the making had a positive effect on Alice Napora, who, when diagnosed with cancer, felt the same devastation and helplessness and anger that everyone experiences in that terrible time. She was able, however, to turn her energy—for surprisingly she found she had more than she had expected—into positive efforts. When she went back to her doctor for checkups, she found that she had a long list of questions, and that her physician often seemed busy and downright brusque. At first, she was hurt and bewildered, then she decided to do something. Encouraged by a friend who had had a similar experience, Alice wrote down every possible question she could think of; then her friend added to the list. Next, the two women checked publications of the American Cancer Society and prepared as many answers as they could. As a next step, they called and wrote letters to various agencies and came upon someone in the state medical association who was willing to talk to them about their questions and their quest for answers. Alice and her friend worked with the state medical association and with doctors in a particular specialty to set up hot lines at certain hours for the purpose of answering patients' questions. The hot lines were often staffed by nurses or nurse practitioners who were highly trained and very responsive to the needs of those who called. Any questions that the nurses or nurse practitioners couldn't handle were referred to a physician, who called back. Around the state, people learned of this call service from brochures available in doctors' offices, hospitals, and clinics.

The instigators of this "Ask the Doctor" program were motivated at first by one thing: their own interests. Because they were so involved, they quickly became the best kind of experts: those who are knowledgeable and eager to share their knowledge—because they had needed it themselves.

Alice's resume has an important paragraph in it, one that led her directly to her next goal.

EXPERIENCE:

Organized "Ask the Doctor" hot line for cancer patients, staffed by nurse practitioners. Worked with national and state medical associations to establish this service for answering patients' questions about cancer. Developed strong research, interviewing, and writing skills in the preparation of document for patients used as a handout in hospitals, clinics, and doctors' offices. Initial distribution of 25,000 copies with more requested in second press run.

Alice is not only living happily ever after, but her zinger gave her the courage—and the entree—to a new full-time job as a copy writer for her local newspaper, which had covered her story and interviewed her early on. Without her unique method of attacking her problem, she would not have been noticed or hired when she was ready to go back to work.

Not all expertise comes from such depths of need and even anguish. Most people become experts in what fascinates them for more joyous reasons.

Take the Tool Man. As a child, Steve Kittredge had spent his first earned money on a yellow-handled screw driver. It was not pretty to look at 40 years later, but Steve still used it. More important, though, Steve had retained his childhood fascination with tools, even though as a bank credit officer he was called on to use them only rarely—for example, when a desk chair broke or a door hinge needed fixing before someone from the maintenance crew could get there. At lunch time he prowled hardware stores, and of course he was in constant demand as a fix-it man at home. "No job too small" seemed to be his motto, and his growing family knew they could count on him for fixing everything. Washing machines and appliances of all sizes were exciting playthings to Steve, and no toy invented had ever stumped him for long, although he had had some close calls on those Christmas Eves when the children had gone to sleep very late. But the toys had always been put together in time to be discovered on Christmas Day—and the added plus was that he then was in a strong position when repair time came, as it inevitably did with children and toys. He had at various times installed plumbing, wiring, new closets, wallpaper, flooring, house siding, roofs, and porches on his suburban house and his summer camp in the mountains. He was a handyman who occasionally sent his automobile to the shop, but only when the large repair manual he bought for each car he owned could no longer instruct him, or when the job required parts and tools he could not get. Neighbors knew of Steve's expertise, of course, and he was generous with his time and advice. He was leery, though, about lending tools.

Long before he began to be concerned about liability, as he came to be, he was loath to lend his precious and helpful toolbox to less skillful workers. But because he owned all the tools needed for most repair work at home, people tended to ask him for help. His workshop took up a very small corner of a small basement, and he had indulged in the luxury of installing an extension phone in it. He was happy to be there many nights and most weekends, and could easily be reached with problems of all kinds. He realized that he could spend more time fixing other people's problems than he did his own, however, and he began to think about his tools, about sharing, and about how he could be useful.

Because of increasing pressure from his teenage children to have access to the telephone, which he was using heavily in giving out advice, he knew he had to act fast. He hit upon the idea that saved him from teenagers' wrath, gave his kids access more often to their telephone lifeline, and gave him more time to be with his wife. He became The Tool Man.

A friend for whom he had fixed many a leaking faucet was in the printing business, and in no time Steve had a supply of business cards:

The Tool Man

Steven Kittredge
5873 North Mountain Avenue
Ashmont, Colorado 23456

Tool Rental and Consulting by Appointment

897-5693

Telephone hours: 8–9 P.M.
Monday through Friday.
Saturday 9–12 A.M.
Sunday 12–3 P.M.

The cards were displayed at the neighborhood variety store and posted on bulletin boards in supermarkets, lumber yards, and hardware stores, and were effective in attracting people willing to pay for his services. He let callers know that he could be called in emergency situations and that he would rent tools for a nominal sum. Steve used the revenue generated to pay for a separate telephone line. The teenagers welcomed this last innovation enthusiastically. He still is unsure about the value of his time as a consultant and, although he has toyed with the idea of becoming a full-time Tool Man, he still reports to Mountain Bank and Trust each morning to consider the value of other business operations and to draw a full-time salary. "Maybe I'll leave the bank when the kids finish college," he muses.

Meanwhile, becoming an expert led to a promotion at the bank, making that steady job seem all the more desirable. Because Steve as banker could draw on his plumbing skills, he was able to knowledgeably evaluate a large plumbing supply wholesaler's inventory. And because he demonstrated his expertise to the general manager who came to the loan office at Mountain Bank, the bank took on a large loan that benefitted both the bank and the plumbing company. When the plumbing supply company was bought by an international conglomerate, its managers recommended that the business continue to use Mountain Bank, and the Number Two bank in town was well on its way to becoming Number One. Steve Kittredge, who had played a major role in that transformation, was promoted. The Tool Man, who thought of himself as a banker first, was gratified to be so noticed and rewarded, and he realized that the job security available at the bank was important to him. His first need was the steady job and not the zinger. But becoming an expert worked for him in ways he never imagined, and he looks forward to early retirement with a pension and an ongoing business in tools and advice.

ARE YOU AN EXPERT?
MAKE A LIST AND FIND OUT

To assess your own expertise, make a list of everything you either enjoy doing or do well. If you are usually calm in a crisis, list it. If you bake bread, list it. If you sing, or string tennis rackets, or make lists, or know baseball players' names and averages, or wax cars, or tell jokes, or draw, or are good with children, or read—write it down. In fact, everything you like should appear on your list. When you make your list, be sure to give yourself credit for whatever pleases you.

Absolutely everything counts here. If you were to list "watching soaps on TV" as something you like, you might have a lot of company. An expert is usually not the only person who likes something enough to be knowledgeable about it. Steve Kittredge was not the only tool expert and handyman in his town, but he was one of them and was willing to share his expertise. Liking afternoon TV dramas is an interest thousands of people share, and it can become a zinger if you use it the right way. Two women who would have put "watching soaps on TV" first on their list became the creators of a famous weekly bulletin that thousands of people buy to find out all the facts on soap operas, their plots, and casts. By doing what came naturally, those women had a real zinger, one that pays them.

Money, however, is not the sole criterion for a successful zinger. It is the idea and the unusual use of it that matters. You should not be constrained in the list you made by thinking that your expertise must be salable. Think of expertise in ways that are useful, not marketable.

For every college applicant there are two parents who believe their achievements are being evaluated also. (Parents again and again are the source of their children's zingers.) No one needs zingers more than high school students who are filling out college applications. Tim Bergen was a student whose middle-aged parents in suburban Milwaukee deserve credit for his zinger, although in the process they could not have known it.

Tim knew a lot about tutoring. He had learned about it the hard way; since second grade his parents and school had been hiring tutors to work with him on his reading skills. Experts of all kinds had told Tim that he was smart, but somehow his school work never quite measured up. He had learned to live with this contradiction, and because of a naturally cheerful disposition he plowed through school until it was his senior year in high school.

Halfway through Tim's sophomore year, his parents had realized that he was an expert. They began to observe that requests for names of tutors who could work on specific study problems were coming to him thick and fast. Because he was outgoing and had friends everywhere, people felt free to draw on his considerable wealth of information on tutoring. His parents did not call it that, but Tim had a zinger.

In December of his sophomore year, Tim sat down, frustrated about answering the same questions again and again. He listed alphabetically all the tutors who had helped him. Then he added the names of all the tutors he knew of, not just the ones interested in reading problems. He had a fairly impressive catalogue before he was through, and he had to list the people by category. "Well," he thought to himself, "I have had to do a lot of that, too." Organizing his work had always been part of the tasks assigned to him.

As soon as winter break was over, Tim tackled the one unfinished part of his task. He called all of the schools in the area for names of tutors. Many were the same names he already had, but no one place had anything approaching the long list Tim had compiled, a list that grew longer with each phone call. By the end of his research, which took only two days of after-school phone calls, Tim's project was complete.

Tim's zinger never made him a cent. He refused to sell his valuable list, although several school administrators offered to pay him when they knew it was available. Instead he distributed it to all the schools who had helped him compile it, to all the tutors he had had over the years, and to any student in his school who came into the counseling office to ask for it. The counselors were overjoyed and handed it out to all their college-bound students, although it was not limited to that group. Tennis pros giving private instruction were listed under the sports heading, typing teachers were there, and so were all the tutors in reading, writing, math, SAT preparation, foreign languages, elementary and secondary subjects. There was almost no activity available to a student between grades 1 and 12—from gymnastics to geometry—that Tim did not cover.

Thanks to a zinger in his application that colleges just could not ignore, Tim was admitted early in his senior year to Brookfield College. College admissions officers were used to evaluating good students who worked very hard and were academically fairly successful. They less often read about students who took a lifetime problem, learned from it, and became an expert. Tim zinged his way in as a regional expert, and he deserved his place in that freshman class.

Parents ought to be aware of times in their children's lives when a zinger will be needed. Parental support for kids' creative undertakings will sooner or later prove worthwhile for both.

Experts, in short, are made, not born. There may be some basic reason for becoming an expert, such as Tim's lifetime academic struggles, which he transformed into a positive factor, or Steve's skill with his hands, which he used as a secondary activity, or Fred's fear of the effects of an environmental problem, which he foresaw as making his future more difficult. But we are all experts in some way. Each of us must recognize our own areas of expertise and think about how to develop them into zingers that will help to achieve some goal.

Becoming an expert means no more than doing what comes very naturally, and doing it more and better and in different places and for other people. Any small area, even ones like cleaning the garage or bowling, can become a field of expertise. Knowing more about less means thoroughly pursuing one avenue of interest so that it can do the most for you in whatever way you need it. Probably no two people will have the same combinations of interests and needs, so you can be the only expert in your town or area. The words "expert in" will look very good on your resume when they're followed by an explanation of the way in which your field of expertise has been helpful to others or has enhanced your own life. We are all experts. Let your list help you recognize that and tell others.

Chapter 3

News That's Print to Fit:
Gaining Credibility
Through Publishing

Martha Freeman was naive, as she freely admits. She thought that staying at home with her first child would be like living in Contentment City. She envisioned a sleeping baby that would coo and smile while Mom went about her housework and made phone calls. Martha had no idea of the demands that would be placed on her by an infant and was not able to continue her computer programming work at home as she had planned. Before she was ready to return to her job full time, she discovered that she was expecting a second baby. This time she was not surprised that two babies were tiring, but she was surprised at the number of phone calls she was making about babies and baby-related subjects.

Martha lived in a suburb of Cleveland and had been accustomed to sharing information with co-workers at the large city bank where she had been employed. One glaring problem with being stuck in the suburbs, she discovered, was that there was not enough child-care information. The Yellow Pages certainly did not cover the subject adequately. In addition, she missed the daily chatter in her office about matters of concern to several people, chief among them, child care.

Combining these two needs, Martha tried out an idea. She found other mothers in her situation and began to publish a local newsletter for parents, particularly new parents. Because she chose to focus regionally, she was able to avoid the pitfall of being too general in her information content. She interviewed pediatricians in the area (and even managed to interview Dr. Spock). She included information about where to find child care, places to take children skiing, support groups for divorced parents, as well as news of broader interest, such as a story on computer technology for children and a description of the perfect birthday party. In less than three years, the publication's mailing list grew from 20,000 to 170,000—with no end in sight.

Martha had not felt a need to enhance her resume; she was in a profession that was in constant demand—but she had done so without realizing it. Her zinger grew out of a personal response to her own needs. It gave her resume a whole new dimension, showing her to be a self-starting manager and innovator as well as an experienced programmer. Her new resume said:

WORK EXPERIENCE: Owner and Managing Editor

Founded *Cleveland Kids,* a weekly newsletter focusing on working parents' child-care needs and interests. Circulation currently 170,000. Written, printed, and distributed by paid part-time staff of four.

Getting published in newspapers is relatively easy. A small paper will even allow you to do a weekly column if you submit a sample article and are interested in an area not already covered. Other places for publication are college alumni magazines, newsletters, specialized magazines, trade and professional journals, and corporate publications (often called "house organs"). Getting your writing published is impressive. It shows that you are creative and have the extra flair needed to figure out how to share your creative projects with others. Best of all, it shows that you can write, a skill in demand in all industries at all levels.

WHAT SHOULD YOU WRITE ABOUT?
WHATEVER YOU KNOW ABOUT

Nancy O'Connor, a college sophomore, was in a different position. She knew that she would need zingers for her resume someday, but she wasn't thinking about that when she called the *Kansas City Ledger* to complain about the lack of coverage of her small college in the paper. The education editor responded to her call. "Send me some news, and if we use it we will pay you $30 a story." That was how Nancy came to be the *Ledger*'s "college correspondent" exactly one week and one story after the call was made. The story proved to be so good that the paper asked her to contribute regularly and even gave her a title. Now her portfolio includes numerous clippings and the following description of this job:

WORK EXPERIENCE: *Kansas City Ledger* College Correspondent.

Submit weekly news stories to *Kansas City Ledger* about campus activities. Write all material and work under deadline. Portfolio of published stories attached.

If you have ever written anything, and you have if you have been through most high schools and almost any college, now is the time to consider what you liked about it. Even if you found writing to be hard work, as it is, list those written pieces that came fairly easily, or were successful at what they attempted to do, or received favorable comment. This is your "What I Have Written" category, and under it you might include a letter to your brother, a report for work, or a college term paper. Next to each item in that list, make a note about why it was successful. This will foster your self-confidence about becoming a free-lance writer. Remember, you do not have to make a living from writing; you're doing it because it interests you and has potential for singling you out as different in a positive way. Being published will bring the acknowledgment you need.

Being a writer is a potentially awesome responsibility, but it should not loom large. If you are writing because you enjoy the act of writing or because you want to share something you know or care about with others, you can give yourself credit for everything you have written and enjoyed. Never mind the Pulitzer prize that you will not win, or the "A" you did not get. If you can write because it is fun and you feel you have something to say, by all means write. Then submit it.

WHO NEEDS IT?
SUBMITTING YOUR WRITING

Think about all of the publications, large and small, that you come across in the course of one week, and make a list of those that could be possible outlets for your creative work. If you arrange your list by subject, as we have done in our sample list that follows, you may find that things fall into place a little easier.

Travel (must have an unusual twist)
   Alumni magazine
   Local paper
Kids (offer helpful ideas)
   Local paper
   Specialized publications for parents
Job-related success story
   Company newsletter
   Union magazine
Hobby, historical interest, family background
   Local paper
   Specialized magazines

DON'T BE INTIMIDATED— IT IS EASIER THAN YOU THINK

"Hi Jack. You free for bowling tonight?" Milt Blair was calling in the afternoon, hoping to find a last-minute stand-in to cover for him on the bowling team. Jack Stauffer did not hesitate. "Great!" he replied readily. "But if I help you out by filling in this time, maybe you can do me a favor. I know you write proposals to management when your purchasing department has some complicated bids to look at. I can't write very well, and I have to write up the charity fund-drive results."

"No problem," replied Milt, "but I can't do it this week. Why don't you write up an outline of what you need to submit, and if it can wait a few days I'll be there."

Jack was willing to wait, and he outlined the main points in his charity-drive report: the number of people in the company he solicited, the number who gave money, and the total amounts, all organized by department. Then he noted that he would need a comparison with last year's results. His final section listed recommendations.

To Jack's surprise when he looked at his yellow lined pad, two pages were almost full. He scratched his head in some bewilderment. "This seemed like such a tough job," he murmured to himself. "But now that I see the outline, the details are easy to fill in." As he read over the outline he saw something else. The report was excellent as far as it went, but it left out an interesting part of the story. More than one person had taken Jack aside and told him a story of his or her reasons for wanting to participate in the charity drive. More people than Jack could have imagined had had problems for which they had received help from one organization or another. They wanted to help quietly to pay back what they had received and were happy to contribute to the drive.

"Why," thought Jack, "I bet these stories would be as interesting to other people as they have been for me. I could add some stories with changes to make them anonymous to the end of the report to make it more readable, more human."

Jack's experience is typical. Writing, which he thought was so hard, seemed to come more easily and naturally once he made an outline. It also seemed to help to talk about it on the telephone with his friend. When the time came to meet with Milt, Jack felt he did not need much further assistance. But they got together anyway after work one night, and the conversation took an unexpected turn.

"I work for the 'Y' in my town," mentioned Milt, "and I think we need to make this kind of report available to the users of the 'Y.' Could you help me put together a little news sheet about 'Y' users and their interests and needs? I'll supply the information on participants and their reasons for using the 'Y'—they list them in the applications for membership. Maybe you could put some of them together with the facts on the sources and uses of 'Y' funds in our town. I think we would do much better in our fund drive for next year if we had real stories about this year's success in terms of the people we serve and the way we use fees and contributions."

Jack, who had never thought of himself as a writer and had even asked for help with a voluntary report, discovered that he liked this idea very much and that he could write after all. The next time he updated his resume he added a paragraph about his reports and, almost more important, clippings of them (with appropriate changes to make it anonymous where necessary). Jack became more interested in nonprofit organizations and, through a reader from the "Y," was offered a career change into a supervisory job at another "Y."

Meet some other real people who, often to their own surprise, have written for publication. In most cases these people are not paid, and many times they do not need the extra credit or pay. Many use the printed word to tell their stories or to provide a useful service. They can say they cared enough to search out publishers and readers, and they have zingers that people at least as talented have overlooked.

Al Fredericks is a dermatologist who never dreamed that he would be on the cover of *Midwest Antiquarian* magazine. (Actually, it was Al's article that made the cover, not Al, who was 42 when it happened—not quite an antique yet.) When Al was in his late 30s, he had finally paid back his medical school loans and was thinking of having a few Saturdays off. He started browsing in an antique shop that was located between his parking lot and his hospital office building. Because he kept hospital hours, many times the shop was closed when he went by, but he found it relaxing to look in the window and think about the various old objects inside. It was his special treat to go into the shop now and then for a few minutes at lunch time, and he struck up a friendship with the owner. After a few months, Al made his first tentative purchase, a small inkwell. It was relatively cheap, Al thought, and he trusted the owner to set a fair price.

The purchase of that inkwell was the inauspicious start of Al's passion and feel for antiques—not to mention his zinger. It wasn't long before he and his wife Becky became owners of some interesting Victorian American pieces. They read books and magazines, and they came to feel confident about telling fakes from the real thing. There were many forgeries in circulation and lots of new furniture were being passed off as antiques, but Al and Becky could tell the difference.

Fueled partly by their interest in recreating the Midwestern past where they, their parents, and their grandparents had grown up, and partly by Al's ability to look at a piece of wood and see more than the untrained eye could see, they became known as connoisseurs around the state. So Al was not surprised one Saturday to receive a call from his local dealer, who had been waiting all week for him to drop in. Would Al be interested in looking at an old farmhouse table? The legs were fat and round, and the lack of grace extended to two large drop leaves that were out of proportion to the legs. Most challenging, though, was an ink stain that was in the wood to stay. No amount of sanding and refinishing in the past had been able to remove it. The dealer wanted either to sell the table to Al as an extra, perhaps for his kids to use for homework as they grew older, or he wanted Al to tell him how to remove the stain so he could sell it at a higher price to someone else.

When Al stopped by to see the table, he brought along his dermatologist's magnifying glass. In the process of looking at skin all day, Al had become proficient at seeing everything, even things his patients and other doctors could not see. He also had his flashlight, and he proceeded to give the farmhouse table a thorough examination. Al was a friend of the dealer, who had been good to him, and he was candid. ''I'd say that this table is exactly what you think it is, an ungainly piece of ready-made oak furniture, if it were not for that one ink stain.'' Intrigued by the stain, Al agreed to buy the gracelessly designed table—primarily so that he could take a look at it in the daylight. His close examination of that table told him what he had not dared to suspect. The ink color, a light blue unlike the normal black and dark blue inks used by almost everyone in the nineteenth century, gave him his first clue. He looked with a more powerful magnifier and saw what he wanted. Scratched in the table under the ink were the initials of a Midwestern artist who had worked for the local newspaper 100 years before. The artist may have had the table in his home or in his studio in a downtown shop. But he was known to have used a sky-blue color in his paintings. The color had faded over the years to the color of the stain. The table was still ungraceful, but it had belonged to a regional figure of some importance, and Al became the owner. Giving due credit to his dealer, he wrote the story for the *Midwest Antiquarian,* and became a regular contributor.

Al could have stopped caring about antiques for anyone but himself, but he was moved to go beyond that and zing for the magazine. The results of his article, aside from giving him a few extra hours of work a month writing about Victorian antiques, included calls from dealers who wanted opinions on wood surfaces and tips from these dealers and others on the location of good pieces of furniture that he was searching for.

When Al needed it a few years later, his zinger was waiting for him. Al grew tired of the daily routine of doctoring as he entered middle age and, especially as his children were leaving home, he felt less motivated to drive himself professionally. He decided to hang out a new shingle and he became

---

AL'S ANTIQUES

Appraisals, Buying, Selling

A second career grew naturally out of his old hobby, and because his contacts were already in place he was launched on his new livelihood with the minimum of marketing needed.

Lillian Ganson was in her late 20s when she developed her important zinger. She had started a new job as a receptionist in a growing high-tech firm. At the time she took the job, her skills were limited to managing the awesome array of phone buttons on her desk set, but after a few months she became extremely knowledgeable about the needs and preferences of almost everyone in the company.

Every day Lillian had to see dozens of salespeople and customers; she had to learn who wanted to see whom and had to decide when to turn people away; she learned the schedules of the managers in the plant and in the offices; she learned about preferences of certain people for calling ABC Cab Company instead of XYZ Company. And, she was often asked for this type of information by ten different people in the course of a day.

In order to keep from spending too much time answering questions, Lillian compiled the most frequently requested information into a catalogue of sorts. She had made lists with names, preferences, phone numbers, hours of availability—a complete internal catalogue of the company's management needs. Because no information on it was confidential, she photocopied the lists, five typed pages, and handed them out to almost everyone in the small firm. "Lillian's List" became a hot item, and everyone wanted a copy and then wanted to add to it or make a suggestion for revisions.

It didn't take long for the personnel office to realize what a gold mine they had in "Lillian's List." They incorporated a revised version in the company's Policies and Procedures Manual and Personnel asked Lillian for her additions when they updated the entire manual. Lillian had her finger on the pulse of the organization, and a few months into her second year on the job, Lillian was promoted to interviewer in the personnel office.

Although she missed her old spot up front, Lillian knew that her zinger, the just-because-it-seemed-helpful idea, was what got her promoted—and might again. She was certain that when she wanted to leave her small company for a larger one, her resume would include an impressive extra accomplishment, one that went way beyond her job description.

PUBLICATION:

Conceived, wrote, edited, and produced an all-purpose information manual for corporate insiders and visitors, including vendors and customers. Included vital information on travel, transportation, local and long-distance communications, internal communications, and helpful information on shopping, eating, child care and other activities in the area.

Meet Tom Rafferty, too. Tom worked as an orderly in a small community hospital serving a wide region in a rural and semi-rural area. He preferred the hospital to the town's other large employer, a large insurance company. He liked being of help, and the insurance jobs made him feel very far from the service nature of insurance; he was not sure that delivering the mail or adding columns of figures all day would give him the satisfaction or the direct relationship with the outside world, with customers, that he wanted.

The hospital was always looking for reliable orderlies, however, and quiet Tom Rafferty seemed just right for one of those spots. He never looked down on his job, one that many young men saw as limiting and not requiring adequate skills. Tom accomplished all the chores required of him in his work and always added some considerate suggestions or comments to patients he met while doing his rounds.

One thing occurred to him as he talked to patients, though. He could not imagine why he always heard the same few questions. It did not occur to him that he was apt to be close to patients without any direct responsibility for their welfare. No one else in daily work on the wards could say that. The doctors were certainly competent, but they were usually rushed. The nurses, mostly thoughtful and considerate, nevertheless also had to administer drugs and often bad news, so they developed the doctors' ways of being caring but slightly distant. They frequently did not have time for the repetitive questions, for the trivia of life in the hospital, for those experiences that were new and often frightening to patients, but were old to hospital workers.

"Why not," Tom thought, "give them something to hold in their hands?" He had in mind a simple question-and-answer sheet to be handed to each new patient who checked in or who came through the emergency room. With help from his girl friend, who had access to a word processor that corrected spelling, and permission from the hospital authorities, Tom came up with a longer version of the list.

Charles County Hospital

Patients' Most Frequently Asked Questions

Q. When can I go home?
A. Your doctor will write orders for you to leave as soon as he or she thinks it is safe. Hospital policy is for patients to stay only as long as they are clearly in need of hospital services.
Q. Do I have to eat this food?
A. Perhaps not, but we will have to check with your doctor first.
Q. Where can I get a hamburger?

A. Wherever you usually do *after you leave.*
Q. Who is in charge?
A. Of you, a specific doctor on the hospital staff. Of the hospital, an experienced hospital administrator who answers to a community-wide board of trustees, including many physicians.
Q. What are visiting hours?
A. You will find a printed list of current visiting hours next to your bed. In case you cannot find it, they are generally 9–11 A.M. and 2–8 P.M., every day.

. . . and so on.

Tom's Q&A was a hit from the day he started it. As the months went by he added to it, with sections especially for children and their parents, for orthopedic patients, and for other special categories.

When Tom was ready to stop pushing stretchers and carting trash, he investigated a new physicians' assistant training program offered at the large metropolitan hospital about 100 miles from his home.

Tom applied for acceptance to the program, which had been extremely popular since its inception. Although he did not rank at the top on grades or test scores, Tom won a place in the very competitive program because of his recommendations from administrators, doctors, and nurses, all of whom were enthusiastic about his way with patients, his obvious care and concern, and most of all his special extra, the patients' Q&A, which was a fixture at Charles County Hospital and had been copied by other hospitals throughout the state.

BREAKING INTO PRINT

After reading the examples listed below, think of the places you could break into print and the things you would like to say to a wider audience.

If You Are a . . .	*You Could Talk about . . .*
Recently single person	Spending the day alone
	Learning new skills
	Cooking
	Investing
	Real Estate
Young parent	Sharing parenting
	Raising active kids
	Small vs. large family
	Getting sleep
Bored employee	Job hunting
	Making the best of it
	Changing careers
	Hobbies

Whoever you are and whatever your experience, you are living at the right time to be heard. Publications abound that will print your ideas—if those ideas are carefully expressed and speak to the concerns of others. Our own interests are usually shared by many others, and editors are eager to fill their pages with material that rings true.

There are many ways of breaking into print, including the easiest route: writing letters to the editor. It is relatively easy to have your opinions printed in smaller or regional papers or magazines; the national ones are more selective in what they print. In addition, "Op Ed" pages are found in most newspapers and are always interested in well-written material, especially if it is of a controversial nature.

All magazines and newspapers have mastheads, and sometimes these include instructions for sending letters or manuscripts. Often you can tell from the titles of the people on the masthead who should get the letter: the executive editor or managing editor almost never should; the features editor often should. If it is feasible, you can call and ask to whom your piece should be mailed.

The kinds of magazines, tabloids, and large newspapers are legion; there is one for every geographic location, hobby, and interest. Large journals that have national and international staffs will probably not be interested in amateur writing, so it would be better to target your piece toward the smaller, special-interest publications. Do not overlook your company's own in-house publication.

To get an idea of the variety of publications, go to a large supermarket, or newsstand. Once you have pinpointed the best market for your story, send a brief and snappy letter outlining your idea to the appropriate editor. The procedures for writing query letters aren't within the scope of this book, but there are plenty of books that tell amateurs how to get their articles published.

The important thing is: if you have a message to share, break into print with it. Each time your material appears in black and white you will gain confidence for the next and you'll have a zinger for your personal or career advancement.

The following books should help you in many of the various phases of writing for publication and breaking into print. Some are geared more toward the process of writing, some to the process of selling your work, and some, like *Writer's Market,* to the process of choosing publications to target for your efforts.

Appelbaum, Judith, and Nancy Evans. *How to Get Happily Published.* New York: New American Library, 1982.

Brady, John. *The Craft of Interviewing.* New York: Random House, 1976.

Cool, Lisa Collier. *How to Write Irresistible Query Letters.* Cincinnati, OH: Writer's Digest, 1987.

Davidson, Jeffrey P. *Blow Your Own Horn: How to Market Yourself and Your Career.* New York: AMACOM Books, 1986.

Deimling, Paula, Ed. *Writer's Market '88.* Cincinnati, OH: Writer's Digest, 1988.

Fulton, Len, and Ellen Ferber, Eds. *Directory of Small Magazine— Press Editors & Publishers* (16th Ed.). Dustbooks, 1985.

Peterson, Franklynn, and Judi Kesselman–Turkel. *The Magazine Writer's Handbook*. Englewood Cliffs, NJ: Prentice-Hall, Inc., 1982.

Zinsser, William. *On Writing Well: An Informal Guide to Writing Nonfiction*. New York: Harper & Row, 1985.

Chapter 4

The American Association
of Astonishing Achievements:
Using Groups to Achieve
Your Goals

The woman who founded MADD (Mothers Against Drunk Drivers) never envisioned that a national organization would result from her efforts, nor did she know that citing it on a resume would constitute a zinger, but both have happened. You don't have to organize a group as large or well known as MADD to make people notice you, however. Hundreds of small, locally organized groups that focus on nonpolitical issues and sponsor a single event have gained recognition for their sponsors. Groups organized around partisan political issues do not make good zingers because of the natural opposition to them by some people. No zinger appeals to everyone equally, and zingers that appeal to one person may turn off another.

The owner of a local hardware store in a small suburb helped the Rotary Club organize the whole town for "Cleanup Day" one April weekend. The following year, the same store owner chaired a committee to organize three towns in a major planting and gardening weekend that has become an annual event.

Others have tackled smaller but no less impressive events, such as organizing biathlons (athletic events using two athletic skills—for example, swimming and running, or biking and running, or cross-country skiing and target shooting—in one race), ultimate Frisbee contests to raise money for charity, Renaissance fairs, or groups to preserve historical customs or activities.

The story of Dick Bristol, who started "Icing Day" one year to demonstrate how ice was farmed and stored in an ice house, is a good example of a zinger that arose, as most do, through his interest in something that he was ready to share. In his Maine home, Dick Bristol was the lucky owner of an old-fashioned icebox, a large chunky piece of ugly oak furniture to some observers. To Dick, however, it represented a piece of the past.

One summer day, as he was browsing through his numerous books and magazines on country living, present and past, he started reading about ice farming. He decided to try to reproduce the life lived 100 years ago. Dick was already familiar with soil farming, blueberry harvesting, and wood stoves (stoked, of course, with wood he cut himself). It was a small step from those activities to ice farming, which involved cutting blocks of ice from his pond and keeping them insulated with sawdust in his ice chest.

The first winter Dick tried ice farming, the major challenge was to cut the blocks into a size small enough to fit in his home-size icebox. He was tempted, like anyone who has ever chopped wood, to make the job go swiftly by cutting large pieces. But when he cut wood for his stove, Dick forced himself to cut stove-size logs. He did the same with the ice blocks so that he wouldn't have to chop and shave the cold cubes after he had lugged them to his back porch and the icebox.

Having preserved his ice blocks through the spring and on into summer, Dick considered another piece of old-fashioned fun, making ice cream. It was no trouble to find and learn to use a hand-cranked ice-cream maker, complete with a steel dasher to lick. For ice, Dick used his hard-won lode from the oak box on the back porch. The friends who helped make the ice cream one August weekend begged to be invited back the following summer, and Dick promised they would be. They also might enjoy, he mentioned, coming in the winter and chopping ice with him. Dick's friends agreed so readily that Dick began to think that other people might like to share his new/old skills, too.

In the quiet town of Belmont, Maine, one Sunday each February was designated Icing Day, and Dick had helpers of all ages who came to gather ice. More ice than Dick could possibly use was harvested, and Dick offered ice blocks to anyone who wanted them. Some people took them home, but others started chiseling away at the blocks with their saws and picks. An instant event was born to go along with Icing Day. Ice sculpture became the activity of many, and the results were photographed and displayed in the Village Store, where admirers of the imaginative ice sculptures gathered to critique the ice animals and buildings that took form from the chunks from Dick's pond.

Icing Day, with participatory cutting, hauling, and in some cases sculpting, turned out to be an activity that drew many people—but not as many as showed up for "Ice Creaming Day" in August. The ice cream tended to vanish more quickly than the ice blocks, but twice a year the town enjoyed gathering for a social event that involved people of all ages. The real end product, of course, was town unity, and when the town meeting came around each March there was greater courtesy and sometimes even more agreement than in the days before Dick's inspiration.

Dick's zinger, events that are still going 17 years later, worked for him when he needed it. Dick entered law school, where the admissions committee was interested in his organizational skills almost as much as his scores on the LSAT exams, and graduated with honors. The imagination and tenacity Dick showed in starting and embellishing a town activity are good qualities in a careful attorney. A Maine city is now the weekday home of Richard Bristol, Esquire, but he returns to his country place on weekends and summer vacations, and participates eagerly in Icing and Ice Creaming Days, which are official town functions.

An existing group may have a broad goal that can become focused on a particular event or activity; for example, the Rotary concentrated on town cleanup and then on gardening. Many of us are already in groups, either at home or at work, whose original function can be expanded or changed in light of a new need. If some particular function of religious social groups, parent-teacher organizations, fraternal groups, or professional societies meets a social need that is ongoing, that in itself is a zinger. Dick Bristol operated on his own, his only obvious organization being his town, which was small enough to be somewhat cohesive and to take over his group's activity.

MADD organized around an idea, not a group, and the whole country paid attention to this national problem. Action for Children's Television was the brainchild of one woman, long an active and articulate spokeswoman for its serious purpose. The content of television programming for children was accepted by most people without question until ACT opened the viewing eyes of concerned parents to the questions surrounding violence and commercial programming for children.

Throughout the last 50 years, labor unions have involved a substantial part of the United States labor force with goals involving improvement of conditions of work for their members. Many of the more enlightened or aggressive unions have also provided services and facilities for members, such as family counseling, recreational places, school advising, and scholarships. These arose to meet members' needs, and frequently they were the inspiration of one person. Alcoholics Anonymous was founded by a businessman who had a need, to overcome alcohol dependence, and formed a group that has successfully helped millions.

Sid Newman was a businessman with quite a different kind of need. He sat at his desk during the week feeling, well, *antsy*. On weekends he was very active with his family; he worked on projects around his house and played volleyball on Saturday mornings or Sunday nights. The days between games left him needing more activity.

As he talked to people in his company, he realized that many of the men and women shared his problem of having extra energy during the week. They agreed that climbing on and off the elevator, picking up the phone, and walking a few blocks for lunch simply wasn't enough exercise. Sid found that many of his co-workers would welcome an athletic diversion at lunch time. So Sid sat down at his word processor and typed out the following memo:

To: Interested Employees

From: Sid Newman

Subject: Mutual Interests

It has come to my attention that there are lots of us at XYZ Company who would like to burn, rather than consume, some calories during lunch. I will be glad to carry the ball, so to speak, for any who want to join a volleyball team. If this works, we may have softball in the spring and summer and other activities. In addition, I understand that there is a movement afoot to start a group concerned about aging parents, and we will entertain any suggestions from the group. Please call me at extension 3210 if you wish to join a group. We tentatively plan to assemble for the first time at the large round table at the far end of the cafeteria next Tuesday, March 10, at noon.

At the end of the first meeting on March 10, attended by 37 people, a group had formed. Representatives from the personnel department were impressed by the diversity of ideas and people, but Sid was excited about having enough people for two sizable volleyball teams. All he lacked was space.

The ABCs (for Athletic and Betterment Committee) were undaunted as they overcame this problem and located lunch-time gym space. The mid-day volleyball games were an instant success, and they are still being played on a regular basis.

But Sid did not stop there. He used the ABC group as a springboard to organize the support group for aging parents. It became a model for other companies to follow as they took on other activities, including support groups for people dealing with dying friends and relatives, for single parents, for working mothers.

Soon other subgroups formed around common interests. Knitting-for-All-Levels is an ongoing group. The Hot-Stove League is active during the end of football season and the middle of baseball season, when members meet around outdoor picnic tables provided by the company and listen to each other second-guess the local team manager's choice of pitcher for the next game. Other seasonal groups organized around the need to share ideas for holiday decorations and gift ideas, for vacation planning, for kids' Halloween costumes, and so on.

The Athletic and Betterment Committee as a group was not a national organization, but it was available throughout the company, in a company that had several plants located within one state. When Sid Newman moved on out of the company, he left an important legacy. And not only was his zinger a boon to the company, but it was a plus on Sid's resume. When he was looking for a new job, his zinger set him apart from his competition. After listing his work experience and education, he had a dynamite paragraph that drew questions from all who read it:

ORGANIZATIONAL EXPERIENCE:

Started ABCs, an employee-managed activity involving 265 employees at all levels of the company. With support from central management, ABCs is the center of groups organized around specialized needs and interests of employees throughout the year. Special letter of commendation from Chairman of the Board and Vice President for Personnel.

Scores of people have seen a need and filled it and thereby have created interesting zingers for themselves when they needed them in later life. For example, in the early 1950s, Dodie Schecter's husband, a manager in a large American company, was transferred to Rome. Dodie had to give up the nursery school she had run in her back yard for 10 years, and she regretted selling the business that had been to dear to her and to her two young sons. But, being the good corporate wife, she did not ask many questions, and off the family went to Italy. After a year of too many company cocktail parties, Dodie was ready for something more. "Something more" eventually became the American Women's Club of Rome, still thriving today. It was and is a home away from home, not only for executive wives but for any expatriate women, who now number in the thousands, in Rome. The zinger here was Dodie's ability to anticipate and act on the needs of other women. She had learned about the organization of the marketplace from her experience in running the nursery school. When she had to uproot again, this time to go to Cairo, she was well on her way to a full-time job with the International Women's Clubs.

It was in the late 1970s that a similar situation arose with an American woman in London who had experience with the Junior League in the New York area. Starting with a nucleus of five American women, the Voluntary Community Service League, as the group was initially known, quickly incorporated British women as well as transient women interested in volunteering. It was the first foreign member of the American Junior League and is now known as the Junior League of London. Maura Rowe, the power behind the original group, has a zinger for her resume that goes far beyond the list of worthwhile volunteer activities. An international service group such as this is impossible to overlook and clearly sets her apart from the people who are simply members of such an organization.

A university is the location of one of the few college-wide celebrations of Chinese New Year each January. A student there missed her close-knit Chinese community in California when she ventured to Pennsylvania to enter college. Susan Chu decided to take matters into her own hands one year and rallied a few friends in her dorm to cook, decorate, and parade in the traditional Chinese manner on New Year's Eve, which generally comes as the second semester is about to get under way. The timing was perfect. People were looking for an excuse to party between semesters, and the American students enjoyed celebrating a New Year twice in the same four-week period. The traditional Chinese food was a treat, too, and as students began to search for authentic Chinese ingredients, shopping excursions became part of the fun for the organizers. The Chinese New Year extravaganza was so enjoyable that Susan had little trouble attracting speakers, who lectured and gave demonstrations. Faculty members joined in the fun and games and made intellectual as well as culinary contributions.

Susan Chu had herself a zinger. Two years later, when it came time to apply to graduate schools, her fluency in Mandarin and a desire to study and teach her own culture were noteworthy items, but the extra zing she showed in organizing an on-going event, not just a one-time extravaganza, made the graduate admissions committee realize that Susan could see a problem through to its completion.

An important component of all on-going groups is a strong common interest among members and a willingness to organize with like-minded people for a worthwhile cause, for discussion, or for mutual support. Creating such groups seems easy, but the imagination and organizational skills are considerable.

Zingers that arise from group involvement are everywhere. The examples above just scratch the surface of the possibilities. You may have been a member of a food co-op, a cooperative child-care organization, or a bookstore co-op. All of these were organized to provide economies to members, and often access to services or products as well. The point is, however, that *membership* in a co-op is not worth mentioning, but *founding* some type of co-op definitely is a zinger.

Opportunities are endless for starting groups. Here are a few suggestions to help you think about categories of groups.

Work- and Job-Related Groups
   Women's workplace issues
   Non-union grievances
   Employee interests
   Buying groups
   Vacation groups
   Exercise groups
   Sports teams

Common Needs or Issues

Political discussion or action
Single parents
Child care
Community improvement
Neighborhood watch

Hobby or Interest Groups

Record collecting
Antiques
Pets
Bird watching
Sports

Although the human animal seems to thrive in groups, there are quiet and self-contained people who have a difficult time even thinking about creating an organizational zinger. However, forming a group can certainly be less socially scary than gaining entrée or leadership in an established group. This is particularly true if you're motivated by the urge to share your experiences with others. Such was the case with David Kellogg. David's college roommates could hardly imagine him founding a group. This quiet and hard-working man was 100% self-supporting through all four years of college, a zinger itself in these days of sky-high tuitions. But his work left little time for socializing. David kept the trials and triumphs of deciphering loan applications and balancing work and study to himself during those four years. Yet, once he was out in "the real world" he found there were others who sought his advice on putting themselves through college. As an assistant in the human resources department at an Oklahoma oil company, David listened to his boss discuss his concerns about meeting the college tuition bill for his son's education. Fueled with pride and the urge to share his hard-won knowledge, David contributed his insights to the conversation. Impressed, his boss arranged a meeting with his son, and the boy's enthusiasm for David's help sparked an idea. Soon David put the call out to others in his area who had put themselves through school and formed a group with the sole purpose of supporting others in that position.

The group David started not only cheers on those in the midst of the challenge, but helps them with financial advice, contacts for part-time jobs, ideas for businesses they might start, and tips for investing the money they have.

At the age of 35, David is the Vice President of Human Resources at the same oil company in Oklahoma and still lists on his resume:

> Founder and Chairman, COLLEGE ON YOUR OWN. After paying costs of all four years at Denison University, created group to support students who needed to do the same. Group sends speakers to area colleges to talk about real stories as inspiration and offers advice and tips on meeting this challenge.

Group zingers can be created by everyone—from the painfully shy to the garrulous. Group zingers are ideal because they can demonstrate your initiative, imagination, and ability to involve others in activities that are worthwhile and long lasting.

Chapter 5

Short-Term Entrepreneurship:
Becoming the Wizard of Your Very Own Oz

"If you want to get attention fast, you can't beat putting 'Founder and President' next to your company name on a resume," says Andrew Edgerton. The words are those of someone who was forced into early retirement at the age of 55 when his company was acquired by a large conglomerate. Carpentry had always been a hobby for the Phoenix aeronautical engineer, and he decided to turn his love of working with wood into a business. He approached a bank with an idea he had already tried out with some neighbors and friends—camouflaging rooftop air-conditioners by constructing latticework fences around the units. He provided photographs of his mini-picket-fences and a marketing piece peppered with the enthusiastic comments of buyers, and the loan officer with whom he spoke found it difficult to turn down his request for seed money. Now, with orders lined up for the next year, our rooftop fencer has decided to employ two additional workers.

Perhaps you are thinking that you could never start a business because you know nothing about finances, accounting, or marketing. Or you think you have no ideas and no time—and you are scared. You have read about entrepreneurs and know they are high-energy people with drive, ambition, and a burning desire to produce a product and work for themselves. And all the entrepreneurs you know are workaholics who always take their business with them wherever they go.

All of this may be true, but we are not talking about starting a full-time business that has to make big money. We are thinking about a business that can be tacked on to the other pieces of your life or that can be done on a small scale—over the summer, during vacation periods, or on weekends. As Andrew Edgerton says, "The best way to start a business is as an adjunct to your existing activities. That way you can make mistakes and you won't be hurt for life. But if you do well, you will look terrific to both yourself and other people."

Actually, you will look terrific just by trying, because the world loves entrepreneurs and the climate always seems to be right for a small business. Part of the love affair with the entrepreneur is the mystique of working for one's self and the desire of so many to do this. We admire anyone who is his or her own boss. We are also captivated by the risk involved, and perhaps envious. Even when we hear about someone whose small business doesn't make it, we still respect that person for going out on a limb and trying. We hope that he or she will try again. There is something very American about individual risk-taking, and our patriotic feelings often well up when we hear an entrepreneur's story.

You are probably still thinking that part-time entrepreneurship is primarily for young people: a high school student looking for adventure, a college kid or graduate student who wants some experience. Maybe you visualize a young adult who tinkers a bit on the side while working at his or her first full-time job. If you believe these are the only people who work for themselves, think again. Here's a look at some real people of all ages who used their short-term entrepreneur zingers for a variety of purposes.

THE ZINGER
AS SOCIAL MOTIVATOR

When a Fort Lauderdale grandmother of four retired from nursing at age 55, she became bored and restless. After her husband died, she decided to start a frozen pastry business. Focusing on the German baked goods she had made for years for family and friends, she took out a loan, got help from the Small Business Administration run by the federal government, and set sail. Her business is still small, although it is growing, but her profits have come from an unusual direction. "I wanted to start in the frozen bakery business because I needed something to keep me busy, and it does that," she says, "but there was a major unexpected bonus. I never used to have much to say to people after church or at the neighborhood parties I attended because my life was pretty small and circumscribed and, frankly, a bit boring. But when I started the business I suddenly had a lot to contribute. It's not that I was just talking about the pastry business to everybody, I had questions to ask people who owned their own businesses, lawyers, accountants; anyone who knew something about small businesses was a person with whom

I wanted to talk. I wasn't the least bit shy, and I learned so much. I've not only created a whole group of friends who are interested in what I'm doing, I've met a wonderful man I'm going to marry in two months. He's a fellow entrepreneur who owns a car wash in our town. It's a business he started when he retired a few years ago. As you can imagine, we have much in common. We've helped each other by sharing names of tax specialists and bankers and gave each other support in the initial stages of getting started—when it's toughest.''

THE ZINGER
AS A MEANS TO ENTER COLLEGE

Sarah Rockwell, a junior at a suburban Long Island high school, was ordinary. She had acceptable grades, was treasurer of the literature club, played on the field hockey team, and worked at a fast-food restaurant 20 hours a week. Sarah needed a zinger, both in her life and to use on her college applications.

Sarah's mother read about a lecture to be given at the high school for parents who wanted to help their offspring get into the college of their choice. What Mrs. Rockwell was told that night was that no matter how good a student's grades and board scores were (and Sarah's were average), applicants needed to distinguish themselves by being unique, because admissions people who spent all day reading applications were easily lulled into seeing the same things on each. If there was a hook in an application, something so different that admissions people would remember it, the chances of getting admitted were much greater.

Sarah was not a hustler, so when her mother came home and suggested they think collectively about a business Sarah could start the teenager was annoyed and unreceptive. However, Mrs. Rockwell kept pushing. None of the plans she suggested appealed to Sarah—until she thought about her daughter's literature interests and came up with the following idea.

She suggested that Sarah write personalized children's stories that incorporated the name of the child for which the story was written. These little tales could be customized using the family's personal computer, and could even be illustrated by a friend of Sarah's who did sketches. Sarah could make up one book as a sample for a child who she took care of to see how it would go over. If it went well, this could be used as a marketing device to take orders for other books. Sarah was somewhat reluctant, envisioning herself as someone who loved the arts and literature rather than as a businessperson, but she went along with the plan, largely to get her mother off her back.

Because she often babysat for a three-year-old boy whose name was Michael, she decided to write the story about him. She created a delightful tale about a child who was afraid of the dark, and generated a surprise ending for solving his problem. Then she typed the story on the PC, printed it on good quality paper, had her friend do the illustrations, and bound the book with staples and colorful tape. She protested when her mother suggested $5 as an appropriate price, thinking that was far too much. But $5 it was ($2 went to her illustrator friend) and, with Michael and his mother as the pleased recipients, word began to spread and Sarah started to take orders.

At first all the orders came from friends of Michael's mother. Then, because business was brisk, Sarah advertised in the local tabloid newspaper under the classifieds. More orders came in. Sarah was busy, she was having fun learning about how to put a customized product on the market, and she was gaining confidence in her own abilities.

When it came time to fill out college applications and write the inevitable essays, Sarah was in top form. She had lots to say in response to all of the questions. In interviews, she was enthusiastic and upbeat. In fact, she began to look forward to her college interviews because she was eager to talk about her book business. After the first two, in which both interviewers were fascinated with her children's stories, she knew she was on to something. Sarah ended with profits of only $45, but got into six of the seven schools to which she applied.

THE ZINGER
AS GRANT PRODUCER

When you are over 60, it's not easy to convince a private foundation or the government to give you a grant to do research or start a project, but that is exactly what Harriet Rowell did in order to get the money to start a Tot Lot in Madison, Wisconsin. A school teacher for many years, Harriet used to spend time in a neighborhood park watching young children try to use the slides, swings, and jungle gyms built for older children. One day she thought about creating a smaller fenced-in area within the park that could contain big-muscle equipment scaled down for use by preschool children. She knew there might be money available for such a project from the government, especially if it somehow involved senior citizens, but she wondered if she would be able to write the grant proposal and get the money, because she had no real experience setting up this type of venture.

She contacted local authorities, who helped her with the paperwork. Although her years of teaching kindergarten were a definite plus, it was the zinger Harriet had up her sleeve that won her the money to start the Tot Lot.

Upon leaving the Madison school system, Harriet had started a traveling science laboratory. Knowing how difficult it was to get good science specimens into classrooms because of the expense, Harriet and three other former teachers bought a variety of kits, such as animal skeletons, pickled organs, and take-apart plastic replicas, and rented them out to schools for a week at a time. Harriet was more interested in bringing the materials into classrooms and making them available to students than she was in making money, but she found there was such a demand that she moved the kits every three days rather than once a week and soon began to realize a profit. She spent an entire year on this venture before bowing out and handing it over to her colleagues, but that was enough to make it count.

In the space on the proposal where she was asked to elaborate upon "a project, job, situation, or activity where you were required to start with only an idea and carry that idea to fruition," she wrote about the traveling science kits. In reviewing her proposal, grants readers focused largely on the science kit business, finding that to be an activity they had not heard about before. The grant committee decided that if she could start up a rental science kit business, she could surely start a Tot Lot.

THE FIRST-JOB ZINGER

When Norm Aronthal applied for his first real job, as a research assistant with a publishing company in Rochester, New York, he wasn't really qualified for the position he was seeking. He lacked some computer skills and had taken only one of the three economics courses that the company required. Many of the students with whom he was competing met the requirements exactly as set forth in the corporate recruiting guidelines. But Norm had a zinger on his resume that he hoped would compensate for his weak computer skills and his elementary knowledge of economics. He knew he could pick up the computer and economics knowledge he was missing, and what he had to give would be difficult to find in the average student. Norm was average when measured by grades, test scores, and extracurricular activities, but he was one of those students who, by his own admission, was better out of the classroom than in it.

Norm had started a tree-pruning business in the summer of his sophomore year and had become a self-taught arborist. He had apprenticed himself to a professional arborist the summer of his freshman year and learned enough to make him feel he could trim, prune, and take down trees. With the blessing of the boss, with whom he had put in long hours learning about how to take care of trees, and with a loan from his parents, he invested in some used equipment and went into partnership with two friends. The professional who had originally taught him the skills needed for tree pruning had business to spare and sent him two jobs to help him get started.

Norm did so well that first summer that he decided to stay with the business through the year. Even though the demand for arborists is slim during Rochester's cold winters, Norm found enough work to keep going by taking care of trees felled by storms. When spring arrived, he returned to the more creative side of the business and was able to repay all of the borrowed capital. By early summer, he knew he wanted out of the tree business and into what he described as "company work." Older people who start businesses after working for someone else often find working for themselves a total joy, while young people who have jumped immediately into a situation where they are their own boss find the idea of working for other people a welcome change.

When Norm showed up for his interview at the publishing company, he quickly brought up the fact that he was lacking some of the desired skills—but just as quickly he launched into the story of his tree-pruning business and what he had learned in the process of that experience. He talked about his skills as a self-starter and his real-world sense of business, and he ended by stating that if he was truly missing any knowledge for the job he would start taking the necessary courses immediately in order to catch up.

The recruiter sitting across the table from Norm was skeptical. He had seen six other candidates that day, all from excellent schools and several with knowledge of two or more computer languages, upper-level economics courses, and plenty of poise. Still, this kid had drive. He also had energy, enthusiasm, ideas, and real business experience. The recruiter was in fact envious. He began to ask more questions. How had this 23-year-old been able to pull off a feat that so few people are able to accomplish? The recruiter finally told Norm that he had the job if he would enroll in an econometric modeling course in the fall. When quizzed about the decision, the recruiter said, "How can you not feel someone is capable when he has run his own business for a year?"

THE ZINGER AS A
STEPPING STONE TO A SECOND CAREER

Not everyone wants to take on the kind of risk, hard work, and stress involved in entrepreneurship. Some second-career people want to relax and enjoy the fruits of their labor. But many others want to move into an activity for which they previously had no time. Such was the case of Paul Cooley, who had raised money for years for the United Way and wanted to help with fund raising at his son's alma mater in Richmond, Virginia. Because he himself was not a college graduate, Paul was reluctant to call the school and suggest he might be able to help. He had heard enough about academic institutions that had snubbed people without diplomas. But his son and a couple of his son's friends persuaded him that he had much to offer a college development office in the way of contacts and savvy. They also convinced Paul that he had something better than a college degree, at least from the standpoint of development work. He had 12 years of experience as a United Way solicitor and, better yet, he had started a shuttle for shoppers several years prior to his retirement. The bus service never made him much money, but it was a boon to the elderly and those who had no cars. The shuttle was also greatly valued by the chamber of commerce in his medium-size southern town because it brought more people downtown to shop. The service offered convenience and comfort and eventually was taken over by the city.

Running a jitney service has little to do with soliciting money for a college, Paul pointed out to his son's friends—but they were insistent. True, the two activities had little in common, except that starting the shuttle demonstrated that Paul had creativity and leadership skills. Eventually, Paul made an appointment with two people in the development office and told them about his desire to help. He mentioned the fact that, while he had no college degree, he had been actively involved in his community. He ran down the list of traditional activities, including the United Way volunteer work, and then he threw in his zinger. He told the story of starting the shopper shuttle and how it had evolved from a private business venture to a city-owned service.

The development office interviewers were intrigued. They wanted more information. Paul came alive in talking about his achievement. He had made very little money on the idea, but he had made a contribution to the city. Soon Paul was happily ensconced for ten hours a week as a volunteer in the development office of his son's college.

A CAVEAT:
SHORT-TERM ENTREPRENEURS
OFTEN ARE NOT GETTING PROMOTED

You may notice that all of the foregoing stories are about people who used their short-term entrepreneurial experience as a zinger to gain entry into a school, a new job, or a new phase of life. None of the people used their zinger to gain a promotion in their present position, and for a good reason.

If you are a person hoping for a promotion and you run a small business of your own on the side that you think might impress your boss, make sure your business is in no way connected to the job you hold. Nothing turns off employers faster than a potential conflict of interest. An entrepreneurial zinger can work best toward a promotion when the content of the work is the same but the target market is different, when the work is done without charge, or when the type of work is completely different from that which is performed on the paid job.

HOW *YOU* CAN BE
A SHORT-TERM ENTREPRENEUR

Although there is only partial agreement about the traits that an entrepreneur must have in order to be successful, the criteria for starting a business are fairly well known. Some of these are necessary for the short-term entrepreneur too, but not all of them. The first of the following two exercises is designed to help you focus on what you really need to create an entrepreneurial zinger and to weed out what you do not need. The second exercise will help you zero in on the type of short-term business you can start.

* * * *

Exercise: What Is an Entrepreneur?

Part A. Problems

Decide whether each of the following statements is **true** or **false.** The answers are discussed in Part B.

1. The short-term entrepreneur can start and run a small business from home without capital.
2. Short-term entrepreneurs must have enormous amounts of energy.
3. If you work for yourself, even as a short-term entrepreneur, you will end up working ten times as hard as you would if you were employed by someone else.
4. A short-term entrepreneur must be single-minded in purpose and must be able to shut out everything else—no distractions.
5. The most ubiquitous trait to be found in entrepreneurs, even short-termers, is the desire to be their own boss.
6. Short-term entrepreneurs all have a terrific idea they're burning to try out.
7. The ability to take risks is absolutely essential for short-term entrepreneurs.
8. Short-term entrepreneurs need to have a clear vision of what the idea is, how it can be transformed into a successful product or service, and what constitutes a reachable market.

Part B. Solutions

    1. **True.** Many service businesses require no capital at all if you are the person providing the service and if you have no overhead or personnel expenses. Other ventures require only small investments of money, often less than $100. Almost all of the businesses mentioned in this chapter had shoestring start-up costs because most were short-term operations that didn't require capital expenditures.
    2. **True.** Because the entrepreneur is responsible for every facet of the business, from sweeping the floor to keeping the books, even the

short-termer or part-timer is going to need energy reserves, and lots of them.

3. **False** or **true,** depending on what you want from your business. If you crave fame, fortune, or the realization of a lifetime goal, then you will have to put in long, strenuous hours. But as a small-scale businessperson, you can pace yourself and put in the number of hours best suited to your lifestyle.

4. **False.** As a short-term entrepreneur, you can keep your side-line venture in its proper perspective. It need not become an obsession.

5. **False.** Short-term entrepreneurs need to be their own boss only for the short length of their project.

6. **False.** Again, short-termers may only be burning to have a good zinger in their repertoire. What sometimes happens, however, is that the activity or business seduces them, and the joy of being on their own takes over.

7. **True.** Even spare-time go-it-aloners need to take initial risks to get started. The risks may not be measured only in monetary terms, but they certainly include time, energy, and resources.

8. **False.** The part-time entrepreneur often starts out with no knowledge of the market or of the usefulness of the product or service.

* * * *

Exercise:
What Type of Business Are You Suited for?

Part A. Lists

Use the following lists of possible entrepreneurial activities as a resource for completing the quiz in Part B.

1. Food-Related Businesses

a. Pushcart
  Ice cream
  Potato skins
  Cookies
  Salads
  Croissants
  Chicken
    wings
  Bagels

b. Delivery
  Pasta
  Soups
  Quiches
  Main-course
    pies
  Coffee, tea
  Fresh fish,
    lobster

c. Parties
  Crepes
  Wine
  Pasta
  Mousses
  Hors d'oeuvres
  Gourmet items
  Jams, preserves
  Cookies, candy
    bars

2. Services

Day care for the elderly
Writing business plans
Market research
Secondhand toys
Firewood
Rental services
Picture framing
Stenciling
Grocery shopping

3. Instruction/Teaching

Aerobics
Calligraphy
Public speaking
Computers
Parenting
Test preparation
  (SATs, other boards)
Tours
Home buying
Financial advice

Part B. Quiz

1. Select from the lists in Part A an activity or topic that interests you. It may be one you know nothing about and with which you have no experience.
2. Does this activity require capital to:
    a. Buy raw materials?
    b. Buy inventory?
    c. Rent space for selling, holding inventory, producing the product, serving clients?
    d. Advertise?
    e. Hire an accountant, lawyer, professional adviser, and so on?

3. List the people and resources that can provide the information, materials, resources, or services that you need to get started.
4. Which of those listed in item 3 above can be obtained free of charge or bartered for?
5. What could you exchange in a barter arrangement to obtain the desired goods or services? (Talents, time, products, other services?)

If this exercise has not led to a brainstorm about what to do, but you are still interested in the possibility of a business of your own, find someone like Andrew Edgerton, the retiree whose story starts this chapter, and make a date to get that person talking. Entrepreneurs, even side-liners, love to tell their stories. Ask around and you should be able to generate a few names. The most difficult part of the task will be getting the person to give you a chunk of time, for these are busy people. Ask for only 15 minutes; you will probably get more, for it is difficult for most people to turn down a request for such a small amount of time, particularly when their own story is being requested.

Chapter 6

If You Can, Do:
Scoring High Marks as a Sometime Teacher

You may have noticed by now that if the achievements people used as zingers were the basis of their 9-to-5 jobs, these same activities would largely go unnoticed. Nowhere is this more true than in the zinger category of teaching. The saying, "those who can, do; those who can't, teach," has been around for a long time. Our society's disrespect, or at best disregard, for the teaching profession is reflected in the salaries we pay teachers. But when teaching is an extra source of income rather than a primary income source, the right course taught to the right population in the right setting suddenly becomes a zinger.

Note the following people:

1. A senior vice president at a major San Francisco bank who teaches high school students figure skating for couples.
2. A homemaker who teaches a course on finances called Money Matters to junior high school kids.
3. An editor who teaches an adult education workshop in the early morning on how to write and produce marketing communications pieces.
4. A computer programmer who teaches a seminar entitled Practical Uses of Computer Spread Sheets to travelers at an airport.

What is happening here? All of these people are teaching in a nontraditional fashion; the course content, audience, time slot, or meeting place is out of the ordinary. None of the course leaders has been trained as a teacher. All are ordinary people who know their material well and are intellectually and emotionally committed to teaching it.

The zingers here are double whammies. Not only are the subjects unusual, the contrast between the teacher and subject gives the zinger more punch yet. John D. Spooner's book *Smart People* (Boston: Little Brown, 1979, p. 45) points out that "contrast is the key to having people respond to you. You give them something that is a total surprise and you have them for good." No one expects a banker in gray pinstripes to play lead guitar with a weekend bar band. If you find one who does, you are intrigued.

HOW THEY DID IT

If you look more closely at the four brief examples of teaching zingers cited above, you will see how the combination of a zinger and a contrast work together. Over the years, the senior vice president at the San Francisco bank and his wife had become a good figure skating pair. They had taken lessons and developed a skating routine that they performed for the local skating club show each year. That in itself is a zinger.

Their decision to work with high school skaters and teach a course in couples skating was the next step in making the zinger even more impressive. The combination of an executive being a good figure skater in addition to sharing his skating expertise with young people made our San Francisco banker special. Larry Hoffman did not decide to teach figure skating because he needed to improve his resume or his life. He is someone who benefits from an achievement and does not even know it is a zinger, much less know why it works. But it does work, and here is how.

One day a group of secretaries eating lunch in the bank cafeteria found out about Larry's skating skills because his secretary, who made the arrangements for his class at the local rink, told several other secretaries that the company had a skating whiz at the senior level.

"What fun! You mean all this time Mr. Hoffman's been cutting figures on the ice with his wife and nobody knew?" asked one of the women in the group.

"Not only that. Now he's going to be teaching a class at the skating club for teenagers who want to develop as pairs skaters," responded Hoffman's secretary, herself surprised at what she had just learned. "I knew that he skated for fun and that once in awhile he did some pairs skating, but I didn't know that he and his wife were good at it. They must be good to be teaching skating to kids— and not just regular figure skating, but skating with a partner."

To this group, the man they only knew as a slick manager and financial hotshot was suddenly more interesting. He was a good figure skater, he did skating routines with his wife, and he was going to teach this skill to young people.

People at all levels were interested. At a meeting in the board room shortly afterwards, another executive at the bank said that he had heard about the skating teacher in their midst and wondered if the editor of the bank's in-house paper wanted to do a story on his skating. She did want to, and she also wanted pictures. Would it be possible for her to go to the rink and capture him in action? After the story appeared, there was even more buzzing.

Larry did not get a promotion, a new job title, or lined curtains for his corner office. But he earned increased respect from many people in his work place who had only known him as a one-dimensional person. He found that his calls were returned more quickly, that smiles and extra courtesy were extended him in the corridors, and that small favors and requests were easily granted. He was a special person to bank employees at all levels.

How about our homemaker turned teacher? Why would a Rhode Island wife and mother who had never taught anything before tackle a subject so foreign to a traditional curriculum? Bobbi Roth was disappointed that her own children's education lacked practical knowledge of economics or finances. "Kids never learn anything about how money works, whether it's how to shop wisely, how to invest, or how to use a bank's services—such as getting a loan, mortgage, or credit line," she told the middle school principal when she approached him with her idea.

The principal was skeptical. Bobbi had no teaching credentials or experience, and the subject did not neatly fit into an already crowded curriculum. Bobbi suggested offering it as a mini-course through the after-school program. She hated to see the financial investments courses in the same curriculum that offered juggling and bicycle repair, but she needed to get her foot in the door. If this were the route, so be it. She produced an outline of a Money Matters course that would run for six weeks, three afternoons a week. It included information normally offered in an introductory course on money and banking for college undergraduates. It was somewhat watered down, of course, but the basics were there and the course was enlivened by Bobbi's enthusiasm, high energy level, and real-life vignettes. By the end of the course, loose change replaced play money for one of the exercises in which seventh and eighth graders in the class learned about interest rates.

Because Bobbi felt she was not going to be able to graduate from college until her two-year-old was eight or ten (after her sophomore year she had married and started a family), teaching Money Matters evolved as an activity that was perfect for her at this stage. It combined volunteering, teaching, and financial information—all strong interests—into a single activity. Eventually, Money Matters moved from an after-school offering to a part of the curriculum on economics, and Bobbi not only taught several sections but acted as course adviser to the curriculum committee.

Here is what her applications contained when she applied to colleges several years later:

> As a community service activity, I designed and taught a course for middle school children entitled "Money Matters," initially an after-school offering that was later incorporated into the economics course at the Baylor Middle School. Money Matters helped seventh and eighth graders learn about investing and helped them understand the relationship of the stock market to American business. Students were taught how to read the financial pages of newspapers and corporate annual reports, how to differentiate types of stocks and bonds, the meaning of speculation, the definition of a tax shelter, and the vocabulary of banking and investing. Evaluations of the course by faculty members with student assessments are attached. Money Matters is currently a part of the social science curriculum at three middle schools in my town.

If Bobbi Roth wants to enter an academic program in teacher training, wants work toward a teaching certificate, or even wants to do another kind of volunteer work in the future, she is a shoo-in. But she'll stand out even if her future college work is totally unrelated to finances or teaching. Her zinger shows her to be a leader, a creator, and a person who will continue to make things happen.

Both Larry Hoffman and Bobbi Roth are not professional educators, but because they know their field and are skilled with people each makes an excellent teacher. We do not expect bankers to teach figure skating or untrained housewives to teach money management, so the contrast between their everyday lives and their teaching activity makes us pay attention.

We come next to an editor who teaches a course in producing better marketing communications materials. What is different here? Well, Marge Beckwith teaches her seminar at 7:00 A.M., a time when most people are just turning off the alarm and starting to open one eye.

Marge was editorial director for the marketing division of a *Fortune* 500 consumer goods company in Columbus, Ohio. She had always wanted to teach a marketing seminar because she knew so much about the subject. She had written some of the snappiest marketing pieces around, including annual reports, shareholder newsletters, sales brochures, and direct-response vehicles, and she felt she had something to offer newer people whose jobs required that they take on these tasks. Knowing that many public relations people were never trained in the art of creating pieces that sell, and because many people had asked for her help she had a strong desire to share her craft.

The first problem she encountered was timing. Daytime was out because of work, and the adult education center where she wanted to launch the course was booked with programs for the next seven months. Marge was not willing to wait. Instead, she decided that if she was really as good at developing marketing pieces as she said she was, she could sell the course in an early-bird time slot, at an hour when she herself was at her best.

She developed a simple, clear brochure to be sent as an enclosure with the adult education center's catalogue. This was a course not only for those who wanted to write punchy sales pieces but for those who were awake and at their freshest early in the morning. Marge suggested that people give up their morning jog or meditation and come instead to three class sessions of two hours each. She would have a continental breakfast on hand.

At first the idea was odd enough to cause the expected reaction—only five people paid tuition and arrived at the center ready to learn something new about marketing communications. But Marge outdid herself with those five students. When it came time to run the course again, this time during the summer, 17 aspiring

sales writers showed up ready to go at 7 A.M. After that, there was
no trouble keeping the course filled. Marge soon found that more
people than one would suspect are energetic at the crack of dawn
and are frustrated by only having evening courses available.

When the adult education center finally had an open slot for a
7:30 P.M. course, Marge turned it down even though she sensed she
might have attracted a larger student audience. She had become so
comfortable with teaching in the early morning and so pleased with
a group of students whose creative juices were flowing when the sun
rose that she decided to hang tight with her odd teaching schedule.

Eventually Marge's hands-on seminar came to the attention of
her boss, via an executive in the company whose neighbor attended
the sessions and reported enormous satisfaction. Marge was asked
about the course in her subsequent performance appraisal. Her su-
pervisor recommended a healthy raise at once, and six months later
put through a promotion for Marge, who now heads her division's
marketing department.

Here is a woman who turned an interesting and very practical
subject into a roll-up-your-sleeves course, and then taught it at an
absurd hour of the day. All of this happened because she could not
teach it at a "normal time." Marge had no teaching experience, no
formal training in putting a course together, and no teaching credentials, but teach she did.

Our last example, the computer programmer who taught a
seminar on spread sheets as part of a series given at O'Hare Airport
in Chicago, is yet another person with no background in teaching
but the knowledge and ability to teach a popular course. Roger
Turabian had successfully taught the course in a more conventional
setting at a community college a year earlier. When the request
came to be a part of a set of experimental offerings at the airport
for travelers who waited hours between flights with time on their
hands, Roger grabbed the chance. There were four original workshops, and this was expanded to six before the whole venture col-
lapsed in a heap from lack of participation. But as we have argued
elsewhere in this book, the emphasis is on doing, on participation,
on leadership and creativity, and not on longevity or success as
measured by either money or a lifetime commitment.

Actually Roger's course was well attended and would have been offered again if the program had carried on. The course Roger developed on creative use of computer spread sheets included a one-hour presentation using an overhead projector and an opportunity for participants to use a portable computer. Roger did not teach beginners how to use spread sheets or get into the specifics of programming within a spread sheet. He merely demonstrated how others had taken their knowledge of various spread-sheet packages and created a range of different and unusual applications. Then he demonstrated some of these on the portable terminal he brought along.

This may sound technical to the uninitiated in the world of computer capabilities, but it was not. Attendees left the sessions with ideas and a broader understanding of what was possible. Many would have to backtrack and learn how to use a spread sheet, and this was not only possible, but expected. The three other courses were also designed to be brief overviews of an interesting topic to business travelers.

Before teaching this seminar, first at the community college and then in the airport series, Roger had never been in a classroom except as a student. But he liked the idea of imparting knowledge, was interested in the topic, and had a great deal of patience with people. He was also extremely knowledgeable about computer spread sheets. He was able to organize his materials quickly, and all four times he taught the seminar he had receptive and pleased groups.

The important point here is that Roger created a course and then taught it in a place where enough interested learners gathered on a regular basis. In this case, the place was highly unorthodox, giving Roger's activity additional pizzazz.

SET YOURSELF APART

Teaching is not always a zinger. It does not zing, for instance, when it is what you do all day, every day, as your main work. It is also not going to attract attention if you teach Sunday school, teach exactly the same subject in the evening that you teach in the daytime, volunteer in your child's classroom, or tutor someone who is deficient in a subject that is your strong suit.

Having just said all that, we could suggest some zingers to turn these non-zingers around. Teaching Sunday school in a prison would qualify. If an art teacher began teaching handicapped people at night, that might qualify, especially if the disabled had incomplete use of their hands. If you volunteer to teach the kind of course Bobbi Roth taught in your child's classroom you would have a zinger, and it would be just as interesting if you came up with a more unusual topic such as how to read tarot cards or do calligraphy or make your own pasta for a family dinner.

To be a potential zinger, the teaching experience must meet one of the following four criteria in order to provide a sharp enough contrast for heads to turn.

1. The teacher's career, personality type, or values are seen by others as decidedly not service-oriented. EXAMPLE: A stockbroker teaching sign language to deaf children.
2. The population that the course is directed toward or marketed for is unusual for that type of course. EXAMPLE: Teaching karate to nuns.
3. The site where the course is taught is not a school, church, or other educational institution. EXAMPLE: Teaching via film or video on a train.
4. The course is taught at an off-beat time. EXAMPLE: Midnight, dawn, noon.

At first you must demonstrate some credentials, in the form of knowledge of or expertise in the topic. Once you have taught a course, workshop, or seminar, you begin to see how relatively easy it is to be acknowledged as a teacher. When you are off and running and have decided that you like teaching, you can take your course on to the next level—an advanced section, a different group of learners, a community college or adult education program.

Even young people have something to teach. One second grader who had worked with kindergartners started teaching her own younger brother his numbers and letters, and had worked her way into his classroom, showing his teacher the flash cards she had made at home for him. Almost on the same day that she first appeared in her brother's classroom, her own teacher and her brother's teacher arranged to have Maria Alvarez help her brother's class. It never would have happened if she had not said, "This is something I want to do." Maria was not a super-bright child, but she was smart enough, and she had a desire to have a different kind of fun.

A slightly older student did a similar kind of activity. Bart Katz came home to Englewood, New Jersey, from his first semester of college at Thanksgiving time and found himself besieged by his younger brother's friends, who needed help applying to colleges. They had all talked to their guidance counselors, parents, and college admissions officers about the how-to's of college applications, but what they really wanted was straight talk and advice on what it was like to go through the process.

Bart was fresh out of the experience. He had applied to nine schools, had gone to visit each, and had lived through the interviews; he had been accepted by six schools, including his first choice. Bart knew a great deal about the process, the experience, and what the first few months of college were all about. He was a perfect target for this younger group of students. They wanted to know everything, but not from an official point of view. Their interest was in the small, hidden details, the side lights of the experience, not the statistics or formal messages most adults give to college-bound students.

Because Bart was both a good talker and a good listener, and because younger students found his comments and advice valuable, the phone rang continuously over the Thanksgiving holiday. Bart decided there must be a way to disseminate the information through a more structured mechanism. He had begun to tire of answering the same old questions again and again. So he called the high school from which he had graduated and asked if he could offer his information as a workshop over the Christmas break.

The school wanted to know more—about how he would present his materials, how it would be advertised, what the focus would be, whether Bart would be willing to suggest reading material in advance to supplement his informal remarks before the workshop started. If Bart agreed to shape the workshop into an approved form, the school would sponsor his course by promoting it for him and giving him a classroom.

Bart agreed and began to work out the details. The course

would be called "How to Apply to, Get Accepted at, and Survive the First Semester in the College of Your Choice." He developed sections on filling out the application, writing essays, visiting campuses, interviewing, and assessing a college during a visit. There was no charge for the workshop.

The course drew a dozen participants, whose enthusiastic response prompted the school to invite Bart back the next year. The second time, Bart coerced a friend into co-teaching with him and making it a double session. They sent out preliminary information during the Thanksgiving break and sent the rest during Christmas vacation. Thirty-two students and several parents came to the second workshop. Out of that experience came a request for a handbook. This pamphlet is ready to go to press, and the course is set to be taught a third time.

Of course, Bart will list the design and teaching of the course on his resume, as he prepares for his senior-year job hunt. He has already included it on a resume used to find summer jobs and it has attracted the attention of each person who has interviewed him. None of his summer jobs has been related to teaching or to the course, but interviewers have all wanted to know more about how he started the course and what he learned from it. Just listing it on a work application has been an asset, because it has prompted much curiosity, especially from the corporate sector. Bart is perceived as a hustler, a person who knows how to make things happen.

FOOD FOR THOUGHT

Teaching can be fertile territory for zingers. To help you come up with your own idea for something to teach, we have pulled together sample offerings from several of the best adult education, community college, and continuing education catalogues to show you the rich variety of teachable topics. As you read through the following lists, think about variations of these courses or workshops that could be taught by you and that could highlight your own particular skills and expertise.

Cooking

Dinner with Only Five Ingredients
Souffle Workshop
Using Phyllo Dough with Skill
New Orleans Food
Light but Delicious Meals
Pizza Workshop
Making Pasta Without a Machine
Indian Cooking
Japanese Vegetarian Cuisine
A Month of Muffins
Wine Tasting for Beginners
Basic Mixology

Computers

Demystifying Computers
What You Need to Know to Buy a Computer
What's Inside Your Computer?
Programming in BASIC
Lotus 1-2-3 for the Office Worker
Introduction to Word Processing

Business

Running a Bed-and-Breakfast
Choosing a Business You Can Love
How to Develop Innovative Business Ideas
Entrepreneurship
Financing a Business with No Money Down
A Legal Primer for Small Businesses
Tele-Marketing for Profit
How to Build a Consulting Practice
Becoming a Skilled Manager
Negotiating Skills
Introduction to Real Estate

Money

Ethical Investing
How You Can Retire in Ten Years by Saving 10 Percent
   per Year
It's Not What You Get, It's What You Keep
Money and Investing
Tax Planning
College Financial Aid

Careers

How to Establish a Day-Care Center
Succeeding in the Restaurant and Catering Business
Interviewing for a Job
The Help-Wanted Ads—Reading Between the Lines
Publicity for Nonprofit Organizations
Changing Careers—For Nurses Only
Housecleaning as a Successful Business

Personal Skills

How to Get Things Done
Goals for Life Changes
Procrastination and How to Deal with It
You Mean I Can Have It All?
The Human Voice
Speaking under Stress
Smoking Your Last Cigarette
Self-Esteem
Creative Change—Getting Unstuck
Body Language and Communication Skills

Psychology

Options for Adoption
How to Stop Worrying
Psyche and Dreams

Coping with Fear and Anxiety
Stress Management
Acting It Out
Approaches to Zen
Psychic Skills
Astrology: A Basic Course

Social Issues

Aging
Introduction to U.S. Foreign Policy
Contemporary Issues
Judaism
India: The Present
How to Travel Around the World with Hardly Any Money
The Woman Traveling Alone

Print, Media, Writing, Literature

Layout and Design
Introduction to Proofreading
Business Writing Made Easier
How to Write a Nonfiction Book
Play Writing
Beginning a Journal
Writing from Your Own Experience
Storytelling

Fine Arts

Designing Your Own Spring Garden
Anyone Can Act
Stand-Up Comedy
Basic Photography
What Camera Should I Buy?
Photography as an Art Form
Video Production Workshop
Film Production

Woodworking and Carpentry
The Best in Chinese Art
Collecting Art on a Shoestring
Knowing Oriental Carpets
Painting from Your Head
Pen and Ink Drawing
Promoting Your Art Successfully
Neon Art
Making Greeting Cards
Shaker, Country, and Appalachian Basket Weaving
T-Shirt Printing for Profit

Languages

Yiddish for Beginners
Spanish for Health-Care Workers
Elementary Russian
Sign Language
English as a Second Language

Music

Appalachian Dulcimer for Beginners
Harmonica Playing
Learning to Play the Penny Whistle
Becoming an Electronic Musician
Sight-Singing
Jazz, Then and Now
When Swing was King
Playing the Recorder for Fun

Health and Sports

Fitness During Pregnancy
Low-Impact Aerobics
Folk Dancing
Greek Dancing
Court Dances of the Renaissance

Hatha Yoga in the Morning
Stress Reduction
Massage for Couples
Postural Alignment
The Inner Game of Racquetball
Bicycle Repair
Roller Skating for Beginners
How to Eat to Win

Mechanics

How to Buy a Car
Home Plumbing for Beginners
Wiring Made Understandable
Commonsense Car Care

Then, of course, there are more traditional courses and workshops that can be adapted for a particular group. An ordinary course in the computer language BASIC can be adapted for fifth graders or senior citizens, as could a course in creative writing. Do not assume that only the exotic or highly specialized offering would be welcomed by a community education program. Start thinking about the teaching angle by looking at what you know and what excites you. It is this combination that makes you the best kind of teacher.

Chapter 7

Home Box Office:
Getting High-Tech Results

Have you ever noticed how closely people listen when you describe a very unusual experience? It does not matter whether you attended the most recent royal wedding or you lived through a minor crisis, such as being locked in an elevator for several hours. Out-of-the-ordinary experiences are relished by most people, and some even regard them as evidence of a full life, although one might raise an eyebrow at that definition. What is beyond question, however, is that an extraordinary event or unusual experience can be turned into a zinger.

You can always talk or write about the things that happen to you, but a far more clever and contemporary way to get mileage out of interesting experiences is to put them into a video. While recording a royal wedding on tape would be difficult, since video cameras probably are not allowed at these events except for use by official photographers, hanging around the crowds that collect on the edges of such an occasion could result in a production many would enjoy and others would find intriguing. No one ever plans to get caught in an elevator, so it is not easy to imagine a taping of this catastrophe. But there is a way to take the subject and turn it into a film or video that could even be salable. The following two examples provide material for workable scenarios.

Nat Hornsby is a sometime video photographer who was on holiday during the week of a royal wedding in England. Nat was actually a recent graduate of Baltimore Commercial Bank's training program and had just started working in the lending department of that bank. Making videos was a hobby, something he spent hours at when he was away from the bank, but not something he could make a living doing. Nat had no invitation to the royal wedding, but he did have his video camera, a piece of equipment without which he rarely traveled.

All eyes were focused on the procession, and on the bride in particular, and Nat zoomed in on the crowd, catching the emotion of the day in their faces and showing only a glimpse of the main event passing in the background. He interviewed dozens of people to find out how they felt about the affair, and gathered a collage of reactions and sentiments. After some careful editing when he got back home, Nat had a very special production with material none of the network documentaries or news pieces covered.

But how could he get mileage from this zinger? Nat had no thought of doing anything other than using the occasion to work in a medium he loved. When he described the video to friends at work, however, several people wanted to see it, and Nat decided to bring it in, announcing in the company newsletter that he would be showing the video in a corner of the cafeteria on a certain day. At the appointed time, the corner was filled with 50 assorted employees, several of whom came away with the distinct impression that Nat Hornsby was a clever and talented person.

Whether Nat was either clever or talented is unclear. What is important is that he appeared to be. Most ordinary people with an interest in video and some basic knowledge of how to work with a camera, how to edit, and how to select an interesting topic could probably have done as well as Nat. But the employees who saw this young person's video of a royal wedding believed that the producer was more than a banker in the making. Nat came across as a person to keep an eye on.

The enthusiasm created by Nat's video made him decide that the endeavor deserved space on his resume. Before, video photography was tucked in with "Other Interests." Now, he created a whole new insert that read:

ADDITIONAL ACTIVITIES:

Created a videotape of the wedding of Prince Andrew and Sarah Ferguson. Focus of the piece is on the crowd's reaction to the royal procession. The video has been shown to several business groups and is available for meetings and social gatherings.

What would your reaction be if, while reading a resume, you stumbled upon this paragraph? Most people would probably be very interested and would want to know more. Nat has indeed been smart to offer this creative work of art to anyone who might want to see it.

A very different kind of experience, but one which also resulted in a video, was that of Juan Melendez, who was stuck in an elevator for two hours in a downtown Minneapolis building. Juan was hardly looking for a career push in the elevator when he stepped aboard, but that was the ultimate result. The 32-year-old media buyer for a major advertising agency was on his way to visit a client when the elevator stopped between floors with two other passengers inside. After the first ten minutes it became clear that the wait for a rescue might take several hours, and the man and woman with Juan began to panic. A firm believer in positive thinking and the power of the unconscious mind, Juan decided to take on the challenge of calming his fellow passengers and getting them to focus on imagining the desired end. After all, there was nothing to be lost and nothing else to do, as he pointed out to Liz and Richard. After initially rejecting his ideas for some group exercises (they thought he was somewhat wacky) they decided to go along with him.

Juan persuaded them to sit down on the floor of the elevator and to relax by using some techniques he had learned in meditating. He then walked them through some guided imagery by having them focus on how they would feel when they got off the elevator. Within 20 minutes, the three were sharing their images, feeling relaxed and optimistic. By the time the elevator was brought down and they were all out, Liz and Richard were expressing gratitude to Juan for his cool head and soothing philosophy.

Whether the imagery worked or not was beside the point. The three passengers spent a calm, controlled hour and a half in a situation and environment that could have produced nightmares in the future.

When the experience was long behind him, Juan thought of other times, especially in the lives of children, when there is apparent cause for panic. He wondered if the idea of teaching children how to relax and focus on breathing and positive images could be the subject for a video that could be used by schools or groups such as the Girl Scouts, Boy Scouts, Four-H Clubs, and others. Conscious of the fact that some might feel there were nontraditional religious overtones to his methodology, Juan deliberately omitted controversial terminology or jargon that might put off parents or teachers.

When the video was complete, he was able to sell it (admittedly for very little money) to an educational publisher. He then brought it to work one day to show to the people in the creative department. Juan, who had wanted to work on the creative side of advertising for over a year, had been unable to convince those people that he had the talent or appropriate skills for their kind of work. He had been on the media side since his graduation from college and had done a good job, but now he had an interesting piece of right-brain activity to show. The creative director was impressed and gave Juan an assignment that he carried out beautifully. He was soon offered a job as creative assistant for two new accounts.

Neither Nat Hornsby nor Juan Melendez had intended to create zingers, but by exposing their videos to others, both had done exactly that—and their careers got a boost, too.

VIDEO APPLICATIONS

The book *How to Get into an Ivy League School* (by Barbara Stahl and Patrick McQuaid) makes a strong case for presenting yourself as unique by describing either on a college application or in an interview an extraordinary experience. The authors tell the story of a student who made a video of his trip to the Soviet Union. The student made copies of the video and distributed them to area high schools, many of which subsequently invited him to speak. He used his zinger to get into every college to which he applied. The same technique can be used for getting ahead in any situation.

The availability of video equipment, both for taping and viewing, plus the relative ease of production has made video a popular creative medium. Videos can be used to make documentaries or instructional or fictional pieces, or simply to record experiences; they can even create personal sales presentations.

Here are some good examples for each of these categories.

Documentaries

Janet Veiro made an hour-long video about coal mining in southeastern Kentucky and began showing it at schools, colleges, and club meetings. When she entered the Lexington, Kentucky job market two years later, she found she was never at a loss for a captivating topic about which to speak. "Every interview became an opportunity to talk about that experience. I'm sure the reason I ended with three offers was because the video proved I could do something creative on my own."

Martin Thatcher was the creator of a video that explored how youth in Japan are different from their elders. Martin, a senior executive from Seattle, hardly needed zingers in his already successful career; but while on vacation in Japan one summer, he decided that, instead of taping ordinary tourist attractions and sights, he would bring back video showing interesting aspects of Japanese culture. He spent several nights interviewing young people in bars and decided to focus on the future of the country. When he shared the final edited version with some of his colleagues, he was invited to speak first at one business luncheon and then at another, and suddenly retirement began to look a lot less bleak. He has ideas for two more videos and he is taking an adult education course to refine his skills in videophotography.

Julie McMahan persuaded the Boston television station where she worked as a lighting and camera director to let her tackle a documentary as a director. After submitting a very low budget proposal for a video that exposed the potential problems of allowing high rise condominiums to be built in Boston's Chinatown, she was told she could prepare a ten-minute piece. After the tape was aired, she was asked to speak at two meetings of the city's Urban Affairs Council. Her confidence grew along the way, and Julie's next step was to apply for a grant to fund an hour-long video about extending one of the major subway lines in Boston; she wanted to focus on how that extension would affect the lives of the neighborhood people. Julie was on her way to making a career change in television from the technical to the creative side.

Instructional Pieces

Helen Wong had always wanted to do a series of cooking videos for kids that would teach them the basics so they could become after-school chefs. Sensing that working parents would appreciate this kind of help in the kitchen, Helen set about the project by having her own kids and their friends play Julia Child. The youngsters prepared such recipes as macaroni and cheese casserole, chocolate chip cookies, Waldorf salad, and omelettes—and Helen got it all on tape. She hoped to eventually sell the tapes to a production company. So far she has had several invitations from schools to show the videos and give workshops. When it came time for Helen to return to work full time, her kids' cooking videos went with her on interviews at hotels and restaurants in northern New Jersey, where she sought a job as a catering manager. She eventually got just such a position—and with it some help toward getting the videos into production. The restaurant's manager happened to have a brother who was well placed in a textbook publishing firm and who was looking for new ideas for instructional videos. He met with Helen and they are now working on just such a project together.

After each of his kids' birthdays, Jack Walker struggled for hours deciphering the printed instructions for putting complicated mechanical toys and electronic gadgets together. A video nut in his off hours, Jack decided to try his hand at offering people a new kind of assistance. He had heard from friends that a specific multi-use workout bicycle was a real bear to put together, so he made a video that actually demonstrated how to do it, step by step. Jack included camera shots from many angles, so that even the most nonmechanical type could come out smelling like a rose. He attempted to sell the video to the manufacturer of the workout machine but was told it would be too expensive to produce for packaging with every machine. However, the manufacturer suggested making it available in every store that sold the equipment. Purchasers could view it there and would remember at least some of the detail, and they could return to the store to review specific parts if they needed to. The idea clicked, and Jack sold it to the producer who took care of store distribution.

Jack was an electrical engineer employed by a large firm on Long Island that made aerospace parts. When his boss heard about the instructional video, he called Jack in to learn more about it. Right then the two of them mapped out a plan for using the idea within their own company. Jack's boss wanted to ship videos to clients as a way to cut down on frequent (and expensive) visits by service reps. The eventual outcome for Jack was a nice promotion, which included responsibilities for developing similar service tapes in the future.

Movies

Abigail Bellito wanted to create a piece of fiction to use as a demo tape to advance her career as a free-lance designer of high-quality local television commercials in Stamford, Connecticut. Convinced that the tapes normally sent to potential clients in major corporations did not demonstrate effectively the full breadth and scope of her talent, she wrote and videotaped a story that showcased both her writing and her video skills. The tape ran for 20 minutes rather than the usual three to five; it was a short story on video. Abigail cleverly tossed into the middle of the script a scene in which the main character watches two commercials on television and then responds to them (one positively and one negatively), thus giving the potential client a lot of information in one video. The tape was a huge hit. Contracts came in swiftly once this zinger was viewed by possible buyers.

Tom Seavy wrote the script and then produced a video about the trials and tribulations of a traveling toy salesman, a job he had held during the summer while in college. A couple of years later, his father, who owned the L.A. toy distributorship where Tom had worked, asked Tom if he could show the video at the annual convention of toy manufacturers and distributors. Tom's dad thought it would lighten up the otherwise boring meetings. The wife of one of the manufacturers, a professional photographer with her own growing studio, was in the audience and was impressed by the video. Tom, who had been struggling to boost his barely-off-the-ground career in photography, suddenly received an attractive job offer and was off and running.

Sales Pitches

When Scott Letterman began his career in a large national residential real estate company, many of his clients were executives who were relocating to Triangle Park, North Carolina, from another part of the country. Scott watched as couple after couple would come into town under pressure to find something suitable in the course of one weekend. Some would spend half of that time poring over pictures and written descriptions in order to determine what they wanted to see. How much more efficient, Scott thought, if clients could look at videotapes of homes meeting the description they had supplied to the broker—before they made the house-buying excursion to North Carolina. With some encouragement from his boss, Scott tried out the idea with the next client who met the criteria for his experiment: a long-distance relocation, a short time to hunt for a house, an adequate budget for just the right house. The first video was somewhat clumsy, but even with less-than-professional camera work, the technique was a hit. The soon-to-be-transferred family arrived with rave reviews; they loved being able to view a wide variety of new houses from the comfort of their own living room, and they made selections about those they wanted to see very quickly. Scott's camera work improved over time, and when sales shot up after the marketing resource became widely used, Scott was made assistant manager of the local franchise.

Heidi Nickerson wanted to get her catering business off the ground with a quick start. She knew that most of her business would come through referrals in her home town of Pittsburgh and would trickle in slowly over time, eventually building to the volume she needed to sustain herself. She pondered about what to do in the interim. She offered two of her early clients a reduced rate if the couple would allow a friend to videotape the food and eating portion of their wedding. This would mean an extra video photographer would be trailing around the edges of the reception, but the couple jumped at the chance to have a superb gourmet buffet for their guests at a modest price. When the video was edited, it showed a beautiful presentation of food, table settings at their most exquisite, and guests happily munching away—in all, a stunning wedding reception thanks largely to Heidi's talent as a caterer. Not only did Heidi use the video to persuade possible party-throwers of her abilities, but she also took it to several bridal fairs, those events where the hawkers of wedding-related products and services gather to entice the betrothed into buying their wares.

Presentation of Self

Because much of what Ned Gerson would do if he were hired as the training director at the Houston branch of a major national insurance company was to make presentations, he decided to have a videotape made of himself in a variety of presentation settings. He included large talks to several hundred people, small workshop presentations, and a number of other teaching formats in between, from round-table discussions for three people to large focus-group exchanges. When he appeared at the last set of interviews, he brought the tape along and left it in the hands of the final interviewer, the man who would be his boss if the job were offered to him. Although Ned hoped to be able to actually sit with the interviewer and make comments during the video, pointing out where the presentation had taken place and who was in the audience, there was no time for this, and the tape was merely presented to the would-be boss. Ned had to hope that it would be viewed. In fact, Ned received the offer without anyone who interviewed him having seen the tape, but it served a very valuable purpose nonetheless. When Ned's new boss, Jim, told his own boss, Frank, about the hiring when he returned from a business trip, Jim was able to show the tape to Frank and say, "This is the guy we just hired." The tape was good; Ned received kudos and Jim was praised for finding a clever and creative new training director.

An Oregon writer named John Scaranoff wanted to do more public speaking about the issues he raised in his books, approaching economics from a nontraditional perspective. He decided to send videotapes of himself in actual speaking situations to a number of campus representatives who were responsible for booking lecturers and speakers. He attributed his increase in engagements directly to this technique. As he says, "I remember serving on a committee in college where we had to generate speakers on a consistent basis, and we were always faced with the dilemma of whether or not to sign someone up whose publicity literature was great, whose topic sounded timely, but who was unknown to us as a speaker. Sometimes these people turned out to be real duds, no matter how exciting the topic. Other times, a well-known person who was an excellent writer would turn out to be a terrible speaker. By using video as a marketing device for selling yourself as a speaker and giving a committee the opportunity to see you in action, the risk is lessened for prospective employers, and the rewards for those having to provide speakers are great.''

Kurt Peterson had a solid track record of proven sales in the high-ticket world of mainframe computers, but when he decided to change the direction of his sales career by applying for a job with Rolls Royce in Miami, he knew that it would be hard to persuade prospective employers that he could make the product switch. He prepared a tape of himself giving a sales presentation to the type of person who might become a Rolls Royce owner. The polish and sophisticated style that came across on the video, along with his other more traditional credentials, won him the job.

GETTING THEM TO
WATCH IT

There are other ways to use videos. Here are some ideas suggested by ordinary people with a knack for creating zingers.

1. Take the video along on job interviews and leave it behind with the interviewer. You do not even have to mention the video until it is time to leave, and then it can be handed over much like a calling card. You will pique the curiosity of those interviewing you and very likely send them scurrying off in search of a viewing machine.
2. Send it with a thank you note after an interview has taken place.
3. Have a reference send the video. When a person who supports a candidate writes an unrequested letter in his or her behalf, that can be very persuasive. Likewise, when a third party sends a video of you or your work with a short note attached, it can be very effective.

4. Send the video as additional supportive material to people responsible for reviewing grant proposals.
5. Send a video in lieu of yourself in situations where you cannot get your foot in the door.
6. Send the videotape to senior-level people in your company to update them on your accomplishments. For instance, if you give a speech to a professional organization, have it videotaped, edit it carefully, and if it is very good send it up to management.
7. Show your creative videos at any available moment in your work setting, at meetings of professional organizations or clubs, at schools, or through continuing education programs.

Videos are fun to watch if they are well done. Unlike printed matter, which can put people off before they even get started, videos seem to make people want to watch immediately. It is a medium with enormous popular appeal.

DISCOVERING OPPORTUNITIES
AND
BEING CREATIVE

Although it is easy to see how to use videos for sales, for teaching presentations, or in situations where creativity is needed, a videotape is probably not the best avenue to use for demonstrating writing or mathematical skills. There are other opportunity areas, though, beyond those mentioned above. Complete the following exercise by creating a scenario for each of the problems; be sure to incorporate use of a videotape in the answer. There are no correct responses, of course, but some creative ideas are suggested in Part B of the exercise.

* * * *

Exercise: Can You Use Videotapes Creatively?

Part A. Problems

1. You apply for a job that requires you to speak French, at least conversationally. How can you demonstrate your fluency in that language to your prospective employer?
2. Your boss asked you to take an upper-level course in economics in order to advance your knowledge in that area. Now she wants to know how you did, beyond what grade you received. What should you do?
3. As a college admissions person, you now want to make a switch to corporate recruiting. You have been told that you will need to demonstrate the ability to interview in a much tougher environment. What type of videotape will get your message across?

Part B. Solutions

1. Bring together one or two or more friends who speak French well and decide upon three separate topics that you can all discuss together in that language. Your choices might be some recent international political event, a course that all of you have taken, a book that all of you have read, or a lecture attended by all. Plan in a general way how to prepare five minutes on tape for each of these segments. Rehearse. Then tape and edit.
2. If you know ahead that this query is coming, you can plan accordingly; if not, you can always stage it later. Ask the instructor if you can give a brief lecture during one class session, perhaps to discuss a difficult theory or the presentation of a case. Be well prepared and know what questions will be asked by the other members of the class. Then have a friend videotape your lecture.
3. Have a video made of yourself interviewing two or three different people for 10 minutes each, or one person for 20 minutes, for positions that are both generic and easily researched. These might be an insurance adjuster, a computer programmer, or a lending officer at a bank. Take the time to research these jobs

thoroughly by talking to people who hold these positions, then ask friends to play the appropriate parts and practice.

* * * *

As you can see, there is a wide range in the use of videos as zingers. They should be thought of as part of your portfolio, either to demonstrate skills or as a sample of creativity. Portfolios, which should be something everyone has, ought to include samples of writing, samples of products, client or customer letters of praise, pictures of accomplishments, audiotapes, and videotapes. This does not mean that you should drag the entire portfolio to every job interview, performance appraisal, or other situation where you have the chance to show off your wares, but it is smart to keep all of these items in one place so that they are available easily. By adding a video zinger to your personal portfolio, you will dramatically increase its value as a tool for getting you noticed.

Chapter 8

Show Business:
Exploiting Radio and TV

After listening to her small-town radio station for years and never hearing a woman's voice, Rebecca Barton, then in her mid-30s, decided that a change was needed. She called the general manager of the station and asked for a meeting in which she proposed that, once a week, she would anchor the station's noon talk show.

The general manager was skeptical but agreed to let her do one show on a trial basis. Rebecca knew it had to be the best show the station had ever aired if she wanted to continue, so she lined up two guests who sat on opposite sides of a hot local issue—taxation to create land banks. Acting as moderator, she steered the discussion through some fiery moments, and the station was flooded with calls. Rebecca got her once-a-week show, then started going on air three times weekly, and eventually anchored her own show five days a week.

She wrote about this zinger when she was applying to graduate MBA programs. The applications included a heading on achievements, which required an essay on "a significant achievement in your life." She also augmented each application with a cassette containing portions of a half dozen different shows. There was no lack of things to talk about in her interviews. Rebecca had shown herself to be a poised, articulate interviewer and a great researcher as well.

USE THE MEDIUM FOR YOUR MESSAGE

Small radio stations often welcome local information to fill air time, and the advent of cable television has brought endless opportunities to people who want to create shows. In fact, local cable stations are eager for people to come forth and fill programming time. Usually, the general manager of a station will suggest that videos be sent directly to his office, although the producer of a particular program may have the ultimate authority in deciding what gets aired. As always, you can find out who you should talk with about your idea or about sending a tape simply by calling the station and asking.

Many adults who create zingers in amateur broadcasting learned about the field by working at college and university radio stations, which are traditional training grounds for people who love broadcasting but may not make it a life's work. Jenna Beauchamp broke the gender barrier when she became the first of many women who were student radio station employees, including one who became station manager. Jen got her job by being very knowledgeable about Big Ten football.

Jen's zinger helped her 10 years later when she was looking for a job with a major midwestern food company. Although by then she had become an expert in cash management and was looking for a position in the financial department, she found her old zinger helped a lot. She had set herself apart, both as someone who could do more than anyone expected at the time and as one who knew more than most people about the territory where she went to college. It did not hurt that she could talk knowledgeably with company executives about Big Ten football, something she had picked up when she was a student broadcaster years before.

A zinger can zing in many ways, but mostly it can open doors. Jen found that interviewing for jobs was a breeze—thanks to the confidence with which she could speak of her radio experience.

Proposing a TV or radio program seems a daunting exercise if you have not tried it. However, it's a natural next step for those who have followed the advice in the previous chapter and created their own video. Most people have had to make proposals of various kinds to many audiences, and the routine is the same for each proposal.

First, you must establish your goals; next, outline the plan you have for meeting the goals; then describe your qualifications for the job. If possible, include a pilot or test example, or at least make one available in the form of an audio- or videotape for radio or TV.

Charlie Woodman was not only an avid golfer, he was a friend to many of the youngsters in his neighborhood. Charlie had retired at age 55 from a 35-year stint as a middle manager in a huge international company, and golfing and friendships occupied much of his time now. He was delighted one day to see a videotape made by his neighbor, Joan Villers, when she had tagged along on a golf outing in which her boys, Charlie, and Charlie's wife, Meg, had all participated.

The golf video proved to be a hot topic of discussion over the weekend among the Woodman and Villers families. They discovered that watching and playing back their good shots and bad ones allowed them to see the strengths and weaknesses of their techniques.

"Why not," suggested Meg Villers, "try to make a teaching video for kids and sell it to our local TV station? Let's ask WNMA to use it as part of its regular programming, one segment a week."

Charlie's 35 years of experience at functioning effectively within a large and bureaucratic company now came in handy. Before they dared approach the TV station, he wanted to organize his thoughts. He knew how to write a report promoting a project, and he outlined his plan for Meg, who was very happy to serve as editorial (and, occasionally, golfing) consultant. Meg suggested a format that Charlie adopted, as follows.

Project Name: "Good Golf"

PURPOSE: Golf instruction for beginning and intermediate golfers ages 12 and up.

METHOD: This is a series of five-minute segments recorded on standard home videotape (one-half inch) that demonstrates techniques of golf to inexperienced players. The series will focus on a different aspect of golf in each segment. Starting with golf techniques, including basic grips and the swing, the lessons will explain how to choose clubs in various situations, outline strategies for different terrain in golf courses, suggest ideas for type of equipment, and discuss places to play golf in the United States and other countries. The total number of segments is 12 (60 minutes actual viewing time); it is possible to combine sequential segments.

PRODUCERS AND CAST: Charles Woodman, amateur golfer (35 years on courses in Southern California, New Mexico, Hawaii, Illinois) and teacher (almost 200 youths between 12 and 18 over 15 years), and Meg Woodman, amateur golfer and editor. Camera work by Joan and Claude Villers. Cast will consist of both students being taught and more experienced players who have been taught by Mr. Woodman.

Charlie's zinger was a success. In a little more than a year, he went from being a retired manager to a speaker and teacher in demand by groups from elementary schools to retirement communities. Charlie was delighted to be working for himself, and not for a multinational organization that required memos in duplicate and that took months to make simple decisions.

Once again, the zingers of Charlie and his crew and of Jenna Beauchamp and Rebecca Barton have a common theme. Each person had a vastly different resume after the zinger activity, and each person stood out from a crowd in a positive way, even though each was not particularly gifted or lucky.

WHAT CAN YOU OFFER? A LOT

To make show business zingers work for you, think about your own interests and options and about the medium that would best show those. Try the following simple exercise, writing the answers on a separate piece of paper. If you are stumped, suggested answers appear in Part B of the exercise.

* * * *

Exercise: Finding the Perfect Role

Part A. Questions

1. What subject or activity do you want to know about that could be answered by hearing a brief explanation or seeing it worked out for you?
2. What are some courses that you have taken, or would like to take, that would help you learn about some interest or activity?
3. What aspect of your home movies could be taken a step farther to become helpful or interesting to others?

Part B. Suggested Answers

1. Auto repairs; radio coverage of local high school athletic events; interviews with local music teachers on radio or video; basic household repairs.
2. How-to guide for word processing; personal financial management; cooking of all kinds.
3. Child care; amateur athletics; video of travel tips.

* * * *

At parties Sonia Mahr described herself to strangers as "just a housewife," until one day she was told to stop belittling herself that way. "What you really do, Sonia," said her neighbor Ron Burchard, "is teach kids computing." "But that's only part time," protested Sonia. "I volunteer in the schools because my kids and their friends need some extra help and because the elementary schools bought all that nice equipment without training enough teachers to use it." "Never mind," said Ron, "from now on you're a computer consultant, period."

Sonia not only learned to call herself a computer consultant to the school system, she experienced a surge in self-confidence. Soon the schools asked her to become a paid elementary system computer expert, and her job became full time just as the last of her three children moved into the middle school. This was fine with Sonia, who began to have more "free" time as her children got older. She soon began videotaping her teaching sessions, much to the delight of the kids involved. But Sonia was concerned that all the time and money spent with cassettes was inefficient.

The end of the story practically tells itself. Sonia's videos of teaching kids to use computers have become classics on the local cable network in her area. She was an experienced elementary school teacher before the computer interest entered her life, and the combination of her early work as a teacher and the courses she had taken to learn and improve upon her computer skills made her aware of the need for course outlines and goals for courses. With this in mind,

Sonia crafted a careful set of plans for her video lessons. "Computers 4 U" became a successful cable series, dedicated to teaching computer use and demonstrating the many applications of computers for children in grades one through eight—and beyond. To the dismay of the school system, a few years later Sonia went to work for a computer company that wanted to focus on the school-age market. Her zinger on the resume told it all to her new employers.

COMPUTER EDUCATION BY VIDEO:

Starting with young children needing computer instruction, created series of video lesson plans for teachers and classroom instruction for pupils. Wrote, directed, and produced videos now used statewide by educational stations.

Cal Stevenson is a trivia buff living in California who turned his hobby, knowing a lot about a little, into a small business, and even appeared on a national TV quiz show. "People seem to think that to be good at trivia, you need a broad base of knowledge, but the opposite is true. Actually, all you need is a limited knowledge in many areas," he told a reporter. He created a high school quiz show for a cable TV company and busied himself spinning off from it a trivia board game. The game made his small company a little money, but—more important—it kept his interest in trivia moving.

His TV show and game were noticed by his full-time employer, a large international consulting firm, and he became the brains behind an in-house trivia contest that is used four or five times a year for corporate outings and seminars. Although his managerial function is in other areas, he knows the various promotions that have come to him are directly related to his early trivia video.

Josh Magee worked for a large company as well, at least until his successful video about starting a new business began to attract attention. Josh spent a lot of restless evenings thinking about being his own boss. He pondered the characteristics that would make him happy and decided he would ask some people.

From casual conversations with neighbors, Josh's video idea began to emerge. He turned conversations into informal interviews conducted and filmed by him. He asked all the questions someone embarking on a new business venture asks: How do you write a business plan? Where should you go for venture capital? How do you create budgets, define, describe, and market the product, budget for the entire operation, prepare accounts?

The end to Josh's story is a surprise. He decided not to become an entrepreneur; his interviews were conducted with people who were chronically rushed and worried, or so it seemed to him. Even those who professed to love their work did not seem to be living the life Josh envisioned for himself. But a senior manager of Josh's company, who viewed the video at an employee meeting, approached Josh about changing directions within the company. He liked the zinger on Josh's resume.

SPECIAL INTERESTS:

Created and produced video series on entrepreneurs for interested employees wishing to start their own businesses. Rental income from videos produces revenues in excess of initial expenses. Over 700 viewers within closed-circuit networks have viewed the series, and demand remains high.

Two personnel managers, Ellen Jackson and Hugh Bernardi, had discussed and analyzed employee grievances over many a business lunch as well as on the job. They genuinely identified with many of the employees bringing them tales of woe, and over the course of eight years they had learned about hearing both sides of questions and sorting out quickly the real problems presented to them.

What better to do, they thought, than go public with some of the problems they heard, sharing them with a radio listening audience. They became, not surprisingly, "The Job Doctors" on a local public radio station. They took call-in questions from listeners and offered advice on issues that did not need legal counsel for definitive answers.

They responded to questions about bosses who are difficult or not very competent or overly demanding or unclear in their goals. They discussed the problem of dealing with workers who bring personal problems to the office or who hinder the productivity of others. They made suggestions about vacations, recommending both where to take them and the extent to which people could structure vacation benefits to their own advantage as employees. They made suggestions about the kinds of benefits that would be needed by young singles without dependents as well as those needed by married people with kids and elderly parents.

The Job Doctors gained a tremendous following in their community and had immediate benefits in their jobs. Fortunately for Ellen and Hugh, but unfortunately for their employer, these benefits translated into better jobs at two different companies. Although their daily sharing of ideas was curtailed, they continued their radio show, and both changed their resumes accordingly.

Not all radio and TV zingers need to involve producing and performing. Public radio and TV stations need all the solid volunteer help they can get. If you are willing to show up on a regular basis, you may become useful at pulling tapes and recordings for on-air performances. You may come up with an idea for a show or be willing to research someone else's idea. If you can promote a particular show at your work place or in your home town, you will probably not be refused some sort of position. The immediate benefits to the radio and television people are obvious. And you will enrich your resume.

OTHER INTERESTS:

Behind-the-scenes research, assistance with performances, publicity for TV science series. Worked in libraries and commercial publications to inform station of implications of science topics prepared for the air.

Radio and especially television were made for problem solving. Communications media, by definition, create opportunities to share thoughts, to instruct, and to learn. How-to courses never fail to attract listeners and viewers, provided the topic is timely. "This Old House" hit the air waves just when interest rates for houses were high and a severe housing shortage was developing in some areas of the country—including the Northeast where the show originated. The show just kept on going and going, and attracted different audiences with a common interest in creating housing on a budget.

Doing it yourself is an idea whose time came with the founding fathers in the United States, but which has taken hold with the freedom to travel and find projects and materials to suit each person's individual need. Restoring and building houses; auto mechanics; needlework; gardening; cooking, whether French, Chinese, American, low-cal, or frugal; parenting—all are topics with great mass appeal that have been addressed, first in small ways and later in more elaborate formats, by individuals who saw a need that television could fill.

There is no reason not to emulate Julia Child and take your neighborhood cooking lessons onto videotape. Calling the show Meals for Meetings would attract parents in cities and suburbs who regularly need to prepare a good meal before an early meeting at school. Most people cannot afford to have a deli cook for them very often, and they want 20 good recipes to bring out for family suppers before PTA meetings, parent conferences, ballet rehearsals, or whatever the school event is. If you know someone who seems to pull this off well, and there are always a few who do, a how-to series of programs using that person's ideas can come alive.

Like all zingers, those using radio and video will come directly from a personal interest of yours. You can choose the medium for your message, but the electronic media of radio and TV have become easier to access and they command the interest of many people. Options for creating video or radio productions are limited only by your imagination.

Chapter 9

The Sorcerer's Apprentice:
Using Internships to Get
Your Foot in the Door

Anyone under 30 who has not done an internship is probably more in the minority than those who have had this experience. For high school and college students of the past decade, internships have become standard, rather than unusual. Apprenticeships offered by companies or politicians are now seen as a necessary opportunity, a way for a young adult to try out work environments, test career possibilities, fatten resumes, make contacts, get solid letters of recommendation, and augment classroom learning with practical experience. The average internship is not zinger material, however, and the population that has tapped into the internship market has been narrow because it caters almost exclusively to students.

If an internship is going to be transformed into a true achievement, one capable of attracting attention, it needs to be a one-of-a-kind experience that *you* create. Carla Taylor, Hugh Fitzgerald, and Sam Lambert were recent college graduates who found unusual internships, the kinds that are apt to turn heads, and all three used their experiences to help in their search for their first full-time jobs. Carla was an assistant to the promotion director of a beauty pageant, Hugh was a gofer in a forensic medicine laboratory, and Sam road-tested and wrote about motorcycles for a trail bike magazine.

All these are unlike typical internships in a senator's office, a store's buying department, or a computer manufacturer's marketing division. These three innovators came up with the ideas for their projects and then identified the place and person who would allow them to undertake the work, persuaded that person he or she would make a contribution, and then went beyond agreed-upon requirements by taking on even more responsibility and eventually having an achievement about which each could talk.

Internships structured by companies, government agencies, or not-for-profit groups may well lack the originality or panache of a project you create. Indianan Carla Taylor, for instance, looked around for something that would allow her to test and further develop her organizational skills, her great eye for detail, and her sense of how big events should be organized. Her peak experience in college had been co-chairing the winter sports weekend, involving the management of dozens of visiting sports teams. She handled it with aplomb, and she also had the time of her life. It was the best combination of pure fun and hard work that she had yet experienced.

125

So the next step was to test it again in a different setting, a new context.

In the month preceding her graduation, Carla checked through the dozens of listings for paid and unpaid internships in both her college's career planning office and the field research center. It didn't take her long to realize that nothing really existed that met all of her requirements. Talking it over with one of the counselors at the center, Carla realized that what the professionals did to generate all of those internships was something she could do on her own. It meant getting on the phone and calling several places that she believed put together big events and finding the one person in that organization who had the authority to say *yes*. But first she had to identify exactly what role she wanted to play in organizing a big event.

The need to be sure of what you want is so important that it requires a few words of explanation. We set forth each day into a world unclear and not at all sure of itself. If you have a vision of what it is you want, it is not too difficult to get it, given the murkiness that surrounds you. Commitment is hard to find and is so admired by most people that things are often handed over without much of a fight, and often with someone's blessing, if you ask for what you want with conviction.

Think about someone knocking at your office door right now and asking to talk to you about an interest this person has in writing a computer program for dyslexic people. The program would teach people how to analyze math problems. Even if it is someone you do not know, you may give her five minutes, if not at that moment then at another time. Perhaps you know absolutely nothing about dyslexic people and their problems. Furthermore, you know even less about computer programs and analyzing math problems in a simple way. In fact, you may be absolutely sure that there is no simple way to analyze any math problem. In other words, there is not a single component in the problem this stranger presents to you that could involve you.

The stranger, however, is very excited about the problem and its possibilities. Without eating into much of your time, she demonstrates so much energy, enthusiasm, and knowledge that although the subject matter holds no personal interest you are drawn in and offer the name of a neighbor who might know someone who has done work in this field.

This is analogous to Carla's situation. She contacted the state coordinator of a small-scale pageant, and from there, through a maze of phone calls, she located the person responsible for the publicity and planning of a larger upcoming pageant. This woman was also in charge of similar tasks for two other state pageants and she welcomed the help of someone whose interests and background meshed with her own. Carla made very little money in the internship and soon learned that beauty pageants were not quite what she had envisioned, but the learning process and the accumulation of experiences were very helpful in future interviews. Carla could discuss with the best of the professionals topics ranging from costumes, chaperones, public relations, media scheduling, and advertising to finding the right master of ceremonies. She had no trouble at all convincing a major hotel to hire her as an assistant to the conventions coordinator, her first full-time job after graduation.

Hugh Fitzgerald never tried to get an internship through established methods. He was not particularly interested in something already set up because he saw that as a position that met only the needs of a company or agency, so he began instead with his *own* needs and tried to determine where they would best be served. Hugh, like Carla, knew just what he wanted. Fascinated for years with forensic medicine, he decided to check it out. He had very little practical knowledge about the field; his superficial knowledge came largely from television shows.

Still, his determination was genuine, and after a few calls to police departments to locate labs in Lansing, Michigan, the area where he lived, he had an appointment to see an officer and talk about his interest. The laboratory where he went for the interview was small and had never taken in student interns. The officer with whom he spoke was less than enthusiastic. What would or could he do in this group? He had no skills or training in the field, so how could he help? There was also the problem of security. Forensic work is largely done under a tight rein of security and secrecy, and Hugh had walked in off the street to talk to the people in this laboratory. There were a dozen problems to be solved before anyone was about to let Hugh into the lab.

Hugh had his work cut out. He listed exactly what had to be done if he were going to get this internship—from designing the project from scratch to outlining tasks that could be done which would not only be helpful to the lab but would be good learning experiences for him. He proposed to deal with the security problem first by having three people who knew him well write letters in his behalf and then by agreeing to sign a letter of confidentiality. There was another round of doubt and hesitation on the part of the laboratory professionals. Hugh continued to call and address their concerns. Finally, because he had worn them down and he was not asking for much more than a chance to observe and run errands, the two officers in charge agreed to let Hugh act as an assistant in their operation.

Hugh learned, to his surprise, that the police work involved was more interesting to him than the forensic medicine work. When he expressed this to the officer with whom he spent the most time, he was quickly introduced to other professionals in the field who gave him a clear understanding of how police work is structured and what divisions handle which cases. He had a much better overview of the field than was possible from any television show.

Today Hugh works for a private detective and is in training to become a private detective himself. The story of his relentless pursuit of the internship at the forensic laboratory combined with a degree in psychology made him an attractive job applicant. His employer, a seasoned pro familiar with all levels of police interaction, was impressed with Hugh because he had never heard of anyone talking their way into a forensic medicine lab before.

The publisher of *Dirt Bike Magazine* had never heard of anyone talking his way into testing motorcycles and writing about them while still in college either, so when Sam Lambert wrote to say he wanted to do just that, the magazine man was puzzled and skeptical. But he knew there were few people around who could both write well and test motorcycles, so he decided to call Sam and find out more.

Sam had taken a couple of motorcycle maintenance courses in the community college in his town one summer, even though he did not own a motorcycle. He had always been fascinated with these machines and, by taking the courses, he had the chance to be around bikes, which became somewhat of a passion once he started taking gears apart. When he read a story in a magazine about a motorcycle test driver whose impressions, results, and thoughts were tape recorded at the end of every day and later transcribed and written up by another person, Sam began to realize that someone who could both understand the mechanics of motorcycles and write about that subject would probably be in demand.

It did not take the publisher long to put Sam in touch with the editor-in-chief of the periodical, and the two were soon striking a deal. Sam would fly to Arizona in the late spring and would be given room and board plus a small living allowance in exchange for road testing the machines and producing seven articles to be published over a period of six months in the magazine. In effect, Sam was to be the literary road expert for the publication.

Because Sam wanted to try his hand in the world of finance by entering a commercial bank's training program, it might be difficult to see how this experience fit into his game plan. As with so many zingers, his enthusiasm and the energy generated around the project created interest. He had interviews with three different banks, and every interviewer had the same questions about the motorcycle project: ''How did you land the internship?'' ''What did you get out of it?'' ''How can you use what you learned in future work?'' ''What does it have to do with working in a commercial bank?'' Sam was ready with answers.

He landed the internship because he was assertive and followed up on an interesting lead. What he got out of the experience, among other things, was the confidence that he could generate his own work, the ability to move easily between the practical world of mechanics and intellectual activity, and the sense that he could work well with many different kinds of people. An intellectual who had garnered his honors in life through academic pursuits, he had also always loved gears and motors. He had wrestled long and hard with this opposing set of strengths. Now, finally, he had brought them together and made them work for him. He knew that he would probably never earn his living from his mechanical aptitude, but he also wanted to make it possible to bring his two interests together in off-hours activities.

It is not difficult to comprehend how and why recent college graduates need internships, and it is probably easy to see what a zinger an internship adds to their resumes. But it may be less obvious why those who have been in the work force for years need internships or how they can go about getting one. However, the internship has proved to be an ideal way for more experienced professionals to test out new careers. Four people who did this are Lee Quinton, Ernie Bennis, Diane Cortland, and Melinda Fremont. These adventurers had very different situations with a few important similarities. None of them called their projects internships. Each felt that the word had a distinctly student-oriented flavor, so they chose instead to describe their experiences as a project, an activity, or even a part-time job. For each of these people, the internship was in some way related to their future work, and all were moving into new terrain. They were adding texture to their lives, rounding out a heretofore single-purpose work life by appending another dimension. That this rounding out was also career related made good sense.

Texture has come to be a word that means diversity and variety; it is the reason liberal arts colleges exist. A major lament of senior managers is the lack of a general education among business majors. "I hate hiring overtrained specialists who only talk business, business, business. They are boring, boring, boring," says a senior manager. Another, whose company does a great deal of international buying, says that he is embarrassed by middle managers who cannot discuss literature, politics, history, or international affairs with overseas clients. A company in Chicago requires personnel beyond a certain junior level to pass a test in which they spend time over dinner in conversation with a top-level executive in the same firm talking about anything but business matters. Those who fail the test are required to take two liberal arts courses at the local university before they are allowed to travel out of the country again.

The four adults already mentioned created internships designed to broaden their horizons. Ernie Bennis was the dean of academic programs at a medium-sized college in Ohio, where for over 12 years he had been both a faculty member in the economics department and an administrator. Having reached the highest level to which he could realistically aspire, Ernie was suffering the kind of burn-out many professional managers experience when they feel hemmed in, with nowhere to go.

While he could not imagine anything at his own or another college that would capture his imagination, he could envision stimulating work in a completely different environment. It was work he had once touched lightly on 10 years before in the state of Tennessee. For three months he had worked there on the tax plan for the state, developing a report on what various tax adjustments would mean to the state's revenues. He had worked directly for the state's director of state revenues department in a research-related project that he used in cases he was generating for a graduate class he intended to teach. The class was never approved, and Ernie became caught up in a number of other projects. He never forgot the excitement of that particular experience, however.

How do you get involved with a major state division at the top levels? Ernie knew he would have to convince the right person at the top for this one. It took him almost a year to identify who that person was and then write the letter that could be followed by a phone call that could then be parlayed into an interview. In government, protocol is crucial.

Eventually it all came together, because Ernie was persistent. He identified, he wrote, he called, he called again, and finally he was granted an interview. In that interview he asked for only a few things and indicated that he was prepared to give much. He wanted an office in the department's section, he wanted access to the data he needed, and he wanted support from the department in the form of interest in his study. He also wanted a free parking space. He was willing to give his time without charge—his abilities, expertise, knowledge, and skills. And, of course, he promised to wrap up the final results of his study both in a presentation to top government people in the department and in a written report.

After almost four months of negotiation, Ernie and the appropriate bureaucrats struck a deal. Ernie would spend one day a week at the agency, where he would have a desk and access to the files he needed. Because he had worked at the college for so long, he was able to convince his boss, the college's president, that he could accomplish his collegiate duties in four days each week and could account for his time at the agency by calling it research. Now that he had the internship worked out, he attacked the project with gusto and soon was able to incorporate his hidden agenda into the project. He hoped to identify full-time work by meeting enough of the people who made decisions and by knowing enough about the subject he was tackling to be sitting in the driver's seat when the happy moment arrived. It arrived sooner than Ernie would have liked, because after an election the new administration took careful stock of Ernie's agency. In addition to some inevitable house cleaning, the new agency head decided that he would target tax reform and new avenues of revenue buildup. The quiet professor who appeared each Friday found himself ushered into the corner office to discuss his findings and recommendations. Within a few weeks, he was offered a full-time job in the new administration.

You do not have to take a day off each week to experience something new in your work life. Lee Quinton stayed within the same corporation and right on the same floor to do his internship. As the director of training for the subsidiary of a growing software manufacturer in Dallas, he experienced a slow time within months of being hired and anticipated that this might happen cyclically. His training responsibilities were directly linked to the company's recruitment program. When the chief financial officer called for a hiring freeze, which happens not infrequently in computer-related businesses, Lee was affected. No hiring meant no one to train. If he had wanted to write the Great American Novel, those slow intervals would have provided the perfect opportunity, but instead he decided to take a risk and raise his hand for work in a new product area. When you volunteer for tasks outside the scope of your job description, there is always a possibility that someone will notice that you are not busy enough. Lee knew that he would probably appear to be under-utilized in his training role, but he was motivated by the opportunity to learn about new product development and to show that he cared enough about the company to pitch in by helping out in an overworked area.

He knew nothing about quality assurance but was quickly trained in the basics of testing data sets and their software environment. The work was tedious, but once he had paid his dues he moved on to the next step, developing a strategy for marketing the new product. This was another area he knew only marginally, but it greatly interested him. He dug in, enlisted the help of the marketing manager and several marketing reps, and did an enormous amount of reading at night. Lee deliberately chose a large number of people to rely on for answering questions and providing support so that he would not monopolize the time of just one person.

Although he had to return to his responsibilities in training well before he had learned all that he wanted to know, he was well grounded in the concepts, the jargon, and the tasks of new product development. When the next lull in training came around, he dove back into the marketing aspect of the product that was now ready to put out to the distributors. After an intense month teaching distributors what they needed to know to sell the product (wasn't this training?) Lee knew more than he had thought possible to pick up in off-hours.

The odd ending to this story is that Lee was not moved into a marketing position within the company, but was hired away by another software house. Feeling confident about his newly acquired skills, Lee applied for a job that combined the old training abilities and the new marketing knowledge. His new employer was impressed with his volunteer work in a different area, his "internship" (although no one ever called it that). If Lee had been a college junior, his involvement would have made him an intern; 100 years ago it would have made him an apprentice.

On the other hand, being called an intern implies importance to many people.

This was certainly true for Diane Cortland, who enrolled in a summer journalism program in New York City with the hope of working as "some kind of editor." Not even sure what this meant, she only knew that she wanted to write professionally—and not at home, laboring alone over a book manuscript. At the end of the journalism course there was a requirement to find an internship where writing and editing consumed 80 percent of the day. Although the journalism program made a half-hearted placement effort to locate sites for the participants in the course, most students ultimately found themselves unearthing their own possibilities.

Diane called and visited several corporate public relations departments to see if the writing done in these divisions was what she wanted. After a half dozen information interviews, it was apparent that writing promotion pieces for corporations and their various products was not what she had in mind. But she did find out that most companies have a newsletter, magazine, or other in-house organ, which offered the opportunity to be creative without having to be technically knowledgeable. Diane offered her services to the editor of one of these newsletters for 10 weeks, 15 hours a week. As a college graduate, a soon-to-be graduate of the journalism course, and a free-lance writer, she had qualifications. What she lacked was work experience.

So it was that Diane came to be the unofficial assistant editor of the 18-page weekly report put out by a major residential real estate corporation with offices in every town in the country with more than 10,000 people. Her job was to collect employee news from the various geographic areas, write up stories, and make some recommendations about what should appear in the paper. She learned about journalism from a practical source, by gathering information, writing, editing, doing layouts and paste-ups, creating headlines and fillers, and even doing a bit of photography from time to time. She was an intern. Or was she the assistant editor of the newsletter?

When the course and internship were over, Diane found a full-time paying job as the assistant editor of a college magazine. From this position she moved up to the editor slot in 18 months. When she talks about the experience of moving from full-time mother and wife to full-time editor of a college magazine, she puts as much emphasis on her ability to pursue and ferret out just the right apprenticeship as she does on the journalistic skills she acquired.

"When I was interviewed for the assistant's job after my internship was over, several of the people with whom I spoke focused again and again on the fact that I was able to find an internship with a big company's newsletter. They kept saying that those places hardly ever take interns and that they rarely work with colleges or community programs to give experiences to those who might want to learn the skills, have exposure to the people, and work in the environment of newsletter production. They wanted to know how I did it, and I told them by doing a lot of leg-work and by presenting

myself as someone who would contribute much to the organization.''

The best internships are rarely posted. They do not usually
exist even in the minds of the people who would benefit most from
having an apprentice. Like the person who wanted to write a computer program to help dyslexic people, the person with an idea for
a unique internship has to knock on a lot of doors, including those
of people who are *un*interested in the idea.

Our last adult intern is Melinda Fremont, who taught third
grade for seven years in Salt Lake City before facing the fact that
her favorite event in teaching was the annual parents' night, when
she stood before her students' parents to explain her approach to
the curriculum and her own teaching methods. She was at her best
on these occasions, making a presentation about a subject to which
she was committed and about which she was an expert. Parents
asked questions, and she could demonstrate her knowledge and skills,
weaving her own philosophy into the answers. Unfortunately, this
opportunity to perform only came once a year.

''I should have been a salesperson,'' she moaned to her room-
mate one night. Almost as soon as she said it, she knew that in fact
the notion of sales, especially sales of some sophisticated product or
service where she could give presentations to clients, sounded perfect. But how to make the switch was her puzzle. If she presented
herself to a company that manufactured a high-ticket product, they
would only see a third-grade teacher who wanted a new career.

Internships in sales are difficult to obtain for two reasons. First
because selling is a very personal activity between two people, and
second because sales often requires performing, and many salespeople only want to perform before the real audience, not before observers. When Melinda approached a friend of a friend who sold
advertising space, she was told that having a third party along to
watch when she visited her accounts would disrupt the relationship.
A second salesperson reported a similar feeling when he told Melinda that she was likely to be turned down by most salespeople. ''I
don't know anyone who relishes having a stranger in the room when
closing a deal. Somehow that would destroy what was going on,
disturb the synergy. You'll have a hard time finding a salesman who

would let you tag along, although I admit that it would be a great way to see sales in its raw state," he told her.

Melinda wondered how anyone ever learned how to sell. She was told about sales courses, workshops, and seminars given by professional training companies. Salespeople were grilled in the theory and then spent hours in mock sales calls, taking turns playing alternately the roles of salesperson, customer, and observer. With each person holding a script in his or her hand, these triads sold phony products and services to each other for hours on end.

Besides being concerned about the expense (fees were usually paid by companies that sent their employees), Melinda was not turned on by the thought of spending a whole week role playing sales of aluminum siding or rust protection for cars. She decided to make a list of exactly what she did want to do and learn during an apprenticeship in sales. Her list included:

1. Attend sales presentations at which professionals pitch sophisticated products and where the audience is large enough so I can slip in unobtrusively.
2. Talk to the presenter afterward to ask questions.
3. Listen in on cold calls.
4. Ask questions of the cold caller afterward.
5. Learn what the follow-up is to cold calls.
6. Witness one-to-one relationship selling in action.

Melinda realized she had been too vague by approaching salespeople and simply asking if she could go along on sales calls with a pro. With a specific list, she easily found several people to help her with every item on her list except number six. But because she had identified and made friends with three good salespeople through the first five goals, she found that videos were available of real sales calls. An insurance company that wanted to help junior salespeople improve videotaped all one-to-one meetings in the office, and, with the permission of the sales manager, she was able to see many of these. In fact, the sales manager, whom she had met through a neighbor who had bought his insurance at this company, sat with her through the viewing of the first half dozen tapes and pointed out what was being done well or poorly.

Within five weeks of having declared that "I should have been a salesperson,'' Melinda had accomplished her goal of learning about sales.

Is what Melinda did an internship? It certainly is if you believe that the goal of apprenticeships is exposure to specific kinds of work, the people who do that work, the environment of that work and maybe, in the best of situations, a good sound letter of recommendation.

This third grade teacher learned that selling computers was what she wanted to do. She learned everything she could about the type of microcomputer that interested her and then presented herself to the company that manufactured that computer. She was hired and immediately entered a training program much like the ones she had scoffed at before designing her internship. This time she was much more willing to tolerate what she had considered to be tedium, largely because she was on board in a sales position—and because her company was footing the bill.

In all of these cases we see examples of assertive skills. For the more timid, we recommend starting an internship search by talking to not-for-profit organizations first, asking for literature about the agency or organization, and then asking to speak to someone who can help you. This may be much less intimidating because nonprofit groups generally want, need, and take on interns. If the thought of going for an information interview makes you nervous, take a friend along; then offer to do the same for him or her. Both of you will learn, whether or not you are interested in your friend's field.

Use the following exercise to generate an internship with zinger qualities.

* * * *

Exercise: Make Your Research Pay Off

1. With the help of the Yellow Pages, city job bank listings, and other literature containing places of employment, make a list of

those companies, agencies, institutions, and organizations that interest you because the work going on there is intriguing.

2. Call the companies and ask for the names of people in the division that interests you.
3. Write to those people and tell them you are interested in a possible internship; say that you will call within a week to set up an appointment.
4. Call and ask for 20 minutes of their time.
5. In that 20-minute interview: Probe for information with open-ended questions; listen carefully and take notes; get the names of at least two other people in similar departments within that or other companies; begin to soft-sell yourself if you really like the place and feel that you could create a unique opportunity for yourself here (no hard sell is necessary yet).
6. Zero in on the place of your choice after several of these interviews and conduct a campaign by sending a letter to emphasize your interest and then following up with a phone call. Remember that after you land your internship the monetary payoff for your efforts may be nonexistent or very slim. However, your internship zinger will definitely pay off in the long term.

Chapter 10

Creative Detectives:
Getting Answers by
Asking All the Right Questions

Only an inept interviewer would not ask John Maxwell about his survey of Rock Springs, Wyoming. John, who wanted to start a business in Rock Springs, was hardly a market researcher. In fact, he was simply a former history major turned part-time insurance salesperson who needed the answer to one question. When he moved west from Ohio after graduating from college, he was tempted by an invitation from a favorite aunt and uncle to stay with them for a while before traveling on to California. A few weeks turned into a whole summer, and soon John was hooked on the Wyoming countryside. By fall, having decided his hard-earned savings would go a lot farther in Rock Springs than in San Francisco, he rented an apartment and set out to see what the local citizenry thought was missing from their mountain community. His goal, to see if he might start his own business there, was simple. His method was, too.

With the help of the Chamber of Commerce, John designed and distributed a survey to 2,500 people in the town and then tallied the results. Unfortunately, John's skills and interests did not lie in the direction of laundromats, gourmet restaurants, or movie theaters. Disappointed but undaunted, he moved on to California, where he sold advertising space for a newspaper for a year before making the decision to go back to business school.

Interviewers at the four graduate schools where he applied were unimpressed with his two routine sales jobs. What interested each school far more was this insertion in his resume under ''Work Experience:''

MARKET RESEARCH:

Designed a questionnaire for citizens in the town of Rock Springs, Wyoming, to determine what services not currently available were most desired by this town's populace. Mailed 2,000 copies, solicited responses from 500 others through supermarket handouts. Determined that most-needed services were: (1) laundromat, (2) gourmet restaurant, (3) second movie theater. Made data available to local newspaper and radio station.

The paragraph prompted a dozen questions. Why had he done the survey? How was it conducted? How had the newspaper and radio station disseminated the information? What had he learned from the experience? Did he want to go into market research? A year after graduating, John still remembers the Rock Springs survey as the item that jumped off the page of his business school applications and created a focal point for discussing his business aspirations.

Surveys can be excellent zingers, if the information is gathered properly, and if the results are written up in a forceful and intriguing manner. Why is a survey a potential zinger? Because the execution of a survey requires entrepreneurial qualities such as initiative, ingenuity, spirit, energy, and creativity—qualities that are hard to demonstrate on a piece of paper but are sought in so many situations. Words alone rarely convey these characteristics, but the right activities often do. Conducting a survey on a vital topic with a specified population around an interesting issue or at a trendy event will gain attention.

CONDUCT YOUR OWN

You do not need to be a statistician to conduct a survey, but you do need to think through the question: What information do I want? (What am I trying to find out?) Write down the question and the answers. John's worksheet looked like this:

QUESTION: What new services, stores, or products would you like to see in Rock Springs that are not now available?

ANSWERS:

Laundromat	239
Gourmet restaurant	210
Second movie theater	137
Other (fewer than 100 responses each)	
Employment agency	72

Babysitting bureau	53
Auto repair shop	48
Backpacking/hiking supplies store	33

A survey like John's may target a population that is somewhat universal, for example, everyone in the town of Rock Springs, or it may focus on a specific subgroup.

Sylvia Williamson thought that asking blacksmiths about their work and lifestyles in a country becoming increasingly driven by technology would make for an interesting story. A high school history teacher hoping to enter law school, she engaged half a dozen students from one of her classes to help. Starting with the name of only one blacksmith, she quickly found eight more, and learned something startling. It is probably easier to get a job as a blacksmith than as a computer programmer. Every blacksmith she spoke with told her that within the past two years each had been approached by a younger person who wanted to learn the trade and each had taken on that person as an apprentice. After a six-month apprenticeship, eight new blacksmiths entered the uncrowded and noncompetitive field of blacksmithing, all to find jobs fairly quickly. This was a terrific story, one Sylvia wrote about on law school applications which asked for a description of an important undertaking the applicant had conceived and undertaken within the past two years.

Broad categories of people, such as senior citizens or yuppies, are not good survey target groups. Focus instead on subgroups— senior citizens who surf, for instance, or yuppies who help organize food banks. Better yet are surveys of new, emerging populations, such as male nurses, Chan Pei dog owners, Yugo drivers, or 12-year-olds who regularly cook supper for their families. Almost anything you find out about the people in these groups probably will be fun, interesting, and newsworthy.

To help you think about a survey you might conduct yourself, start by understanding that you do not have to do something technically accurate to use survey results for a zinger. If you want to carry off a highly professional survey, there are plenty of sources to be found at any good college or university library which will help you do this, but it is unnecessary for zinger purposes. In fact, a survey that is too scientific may not work at all as a zinger. A dissertation entitled "A Comparison of Rural Farmers in Two Louisiana Counties" simply does not zing. However, if you carefully target the right audience, you will have a winner.

Liz Bachman was a Pennsylvania housewife who compared train service with bus service and then wrote it up on a job application. Let her tell the story.

"We could not decide whether to buy a house in Penfield or Lancaster—one was on the train line and one on the bus line. So I decided to hang around the train station one morning and ask everyone getting on if the service was good. Then I did the same at the bus station. It may not have been very scientific, but we got the picture. The bus won by a mile, or by 20 minutes. We bought the Penfield house, and then I decided to write the whole thing up and send it on to every realtor in Penfield. Two years later they're still quoting me in their literature."

Her resume looked like this:

SURVEY RESEARCH:

Designed a brief questionnaire used to determine whether transportation by train or bus was more valued by commuters in Lancaster County, Pennsylvania. Using a random sample of 50 commuters polled at both the train and bus stations, gathered and analyzed data. Released information to realtors and local newspapers. Photocopies of clippings attached.

The job for which she applied was hers, not only because she had the expected skills and talents, but because her zinger at the end of the resume set her apart from all other applicants.

To get you thinking about the possibility of doing a survey of a targeted population and using it for a zinger, the following exercise should be helpful. You may find it useful to sit down with a friend and answer the questions, as brainstorming is often more fruitful with two or more people.

*   *   *   *

Exercise: Let Free Association Lead You to Your Target Population

1. In the left-hand column is a list of major attributes for grouping people. In the right-hand column is a list of categories (with examples) that give character and personality to the variables in the first column. Add your own items to both columns, being creative with your choices.

Major Variables

Age _____
Sex _____
Race _____
Geography _____
Occupation _____
Education _____
Marital status _____
Physical attributes _____
Religion _____
Other

Minor Variables

Interests (Listening to jazz)
Hobbies (Making and flying kites)
Athletics (Boxing, wind-surfing)
Behavior (Nonsmoking, cheerful)
Beliefs, values (Friendships)
Responsibilities (Care of parent)
Possessions (Home computer)
Other _____

2. Combine variables from both columns to create new categories. Be imaginative. The goal is to be as free with your thoughts as possible. For example, here are three new categories formed by this type of free association:

   a. Women who box.
   b. California police who use karate to manage street gangs.
   c. Single men who raise children.

3. Where might you find one person in each of the above groups? Call or write professional or social organizations that might have the people you are looking for as members. For example:

   a. Women who box: Call a local boxing club or group for names of female members.
   b. California police who use karate: Call a karate school in

Los Angeles; call or write an East Los Angeles police station.
c. Single men who raise children: Write and call single-par-
ents groups run by social, religious, and educational organizations.

* * * *

At first it might appear difficult to locate the sample population
you are looking for, but sometimes you need to find only a few
people in the category to conduct a good survey. In Sylvia Williamson's survey of blacksmiths, the focus was on an occupational category, with no selection from the personality column. Your choice of
a population can be simple or complex. The goal is to find an interesting story. If you find an interesting group of people with whom
to talk, and you address issues that matter, your story will practically write itself.

Several years ago, when interest rates on loans rose to 20 percent, Scott Millstead, who worked as a junior member of a consulting firm that did economic forecasting, thought it would be
instructive to look at how the people in his own company were affected by tight money. Everyone knew home buying was down, but
most of the people in his professional company already owned
homes. Scott was curious about the impact on relatively affluent
people, so he constructed a sample of upper-, middle-, and lower-
level managers and surveyed them. The findings showed that, at all
levels, there had been a definite impact. Even top-level executives
with high salaries, many of whom lived in expensive houses, were
holding off on the purchase of a boat or country house.

Scott pulled together enough data for an article and sent it off
to a local paper. A month later, the *Wall Street Journal* carried a story
on rising interest rates and quoted from Scott's story the news that
forecasters do believe their own predictions and act on them. What
did this do for Scott and his career? A year later, after contacting
three leading investment banks in New York, Scott found himself
talking in interviews about the survey, the article, and the *Journal*

quote. "I can't say the reason I got two offers was because of this, but it made the interviews fun to go through, unlike the ones I had right after I got my MBA. Of course, I had a lot to say about my work too, but the survey was a practical, down-to-earth project that was interesting for me. It lightened the usual heavy tone that weighs down most interviews in the financial community and it made me feel more relaxed."

Instead of focusing on a population, this survey centered on an issue, sky-high interest rates. Survey issues can be national ones that everyone is aware of, or local ones of importance to people in a smaller community, state, or region. Big issues need to be localized for one person to manage and to attract the interest of a hometown newspaper or radio station. Whether it is nuclear power, prison reform, terrorism, or the value of the U.S. dollar, the thrust should be local: How are citizens in the community affected? Who in the town or city is involved personally?

Andrea Keeler used an idea she stole from another town to do a survey of her own community. "Landbanking" was the term used by local government officials on Manatee Island, a small but very desirable island increasingly devoted to vacationers, to keep a percentage of open fields and forests from developers' hands. Landbanking required new house buyers to pay a 2 percent tax to the town when they bought their houses; that amount was pooled and used by the town to buy up open spaces and conserve them. Andrea researched how the idea had gained momentum and had eventually become law. She then constructed a survey to use in her home town of Eastham, New Hampshire. She found enormous support for landbanking and she took her findings to her town's planning board. As a result an ordinance was passed, and Andrea ran successfully for town council the next year.

The best place to begin researching for an issues-oriented survey is with big-city and local newspapers and weekly newsmagazines. An exercise to help you begin this task follows.

* * * *

Exercise: Is *Your* Issue on the Front Page?

With a Sunday *New York Times* or a copy of *Time, Newsweek,* or *Business Week* in hand, jot down the major issues in the following categories.

  1. What four national issues are currently most newsworthy?

  2. What two or three major international issues are current?

  3. Find at least one issue that falls in each of the following categories.
     a. Business
     b. Sports
     c. Theater and arts
     d. Literature
     e. Government

  4. Pick at least two of the issues listed above and think about ways they could be related to your own state, region, town, neighborhood, work place, college, or family. Then make a list of questions connecting the issue to the local populace.

*   *   *   *

With this exercise in hand you can focus your thinking on the issues that interest you; the previous exercise helped you think about groups that would be interesting to survey. In addition to targeting a specific group or finding issues that matter, it is possible to structure an interview around a location and to change ordinary places into extraordinary experiences.

ORDINARY PLACES—
EXTRAORDINARY SURVEYS

When the boredom of a week-long hospital stay finally got to Hank Domini, he decided to pop into the rooms on his floor and ask patients what they thought of the new ruling allowing nurses and other hospital employees to wear street clothes rather than uniforms to work. This major teaching hospital of a large university in the Northeast was the first to take such a dramatic step, and Hank found reactions to it interesting and amusing. He did not have a survey in mind as he set out on his informal rounds, but as he talked to people he realized the topic was a hot one, at least for the patients. Not wanting to bring a notebook and pencil for fear of appearing too much like a newspaper reporter, he would wheel himself back to his room after each chat and jot down notes before proceeding to the next person.

His results showed that people of all ages found the lack of uniforms confusing. The patients on his floor said they could no longer distinguish visitors from nurses and were thrown off by this. Some even called it unprofessional. In the pediatric wing, Hank found more of the same. Many of the people on his floor were elderly and somewhat traditional, and their responses were, to him, predictable. But he was surprised to learn that younger patients were just as unsettled as older ones.

On the day Hank was released, he shared with his doctor a graph he had made showing his findings. The doctor suggested writing the whole thing up and submitting it to the hospital employee newsletter. After the publication of his story, Hank was asked to speak to nurses and other hospital workers to find out their thoughts about the policy. Soon the editor of a magazine for hospital administrators asked Hank to write a more lengthy article on the subject.

The interesting twist to this story is that Hank was not looking for another job, a place in graduate school, a move up the ladder, or a boost to his social life. A 62-year-old retired AT&T manager, he did not need events that called attention to his life. But he had been considering ways to become involved with small businesses in his community in some kind of advisory role. In his application to SCORE, the association that connects retired people with individual companies, he discussed his hospital survey. Previously anxious about the fact that he was not exactly an executive (SCORE stands for Senior Corps of Retired Executives), he had wondered if he would be an acceptable candidate. His confidence was heightened by the survey, and during his interview he spoke with such enthusiasm and knowledge about the subject that there was no question about his ability to serve as a SCORE adviser.

People who are already gathered in places like supermarkets, schools, hospitals, churches, or group meetings are a captive audience for questions connected in some way to that environment. The trick is to find a topic that will pique people's interest. A good supermarket topic might focus on the quality of brandless or generic products. In high schools, a hot subject concerns what IQ tests or SAT exams really measure. This never goes out of date. Topics totally unrelated to the survey environment are legitimate too. A supermarket survey could focus on a local political issue as well.

You will guarantee a 100 percent return by attending an event where the group you would like to question is present. If you want to learn the post-graduation plans of a college's senior class, for instance, show up at the rehearsal for commencement and, when everyone is lined up, simply walk down the line yourself checking off answers in boxes. Mailing a questionnaire to the same group of people will never get more than a 40 percent return, and it will take weeks. Even though the results may be interesting, the technique itself is unusual enough to be a zinger. This person could have written up something publishable on unusual but highly successful survey methods.

Can you think of a topic for each of the following places that could be used as the basis for an informal survey?

School
Library
Bank
Town hall
Grocery store
Pharmacy
Police station

Dump or
    transfer station
Historical society
Scout headquarters
Taxi stand
Bus station
Other

Events offer opportunities for pulling together opinion data also. Fairs, parades, rock concerts, town meetings, political rallies, and company picnics bring out large numbers of people, most of whom would not mind answering a question or two about a topic of interest to them. Times Square on New Year's Eve is a challenge, but if you are up for it you could ask a single question of 100 people on a year-end topic and possibly come up with some lively material. Imagine yourself as this person:

OPINION POLLER:

Designed a field questionnaire for use with New Year's Eve celebrants in Times Square. Randomly selected 100 people and asked about their choice of the year's top newsmaker. Tallied and analyzed results, which were published in five New York newspapers. Clippings available.

Whether your credentials are impeccable or completely non-existent, most readers or interviewers would be curious to know more about the results, the methodology, or the purpose of this survey. And you, the opinion poller, have an intriguing story to tell.

SPREADING THE WORD

The actual use of the survey data is up to you, depending on what you want to get out of the exercise, how thorough a job you did, and what you found out. Start with this last item first. A small informal survey will usually not net any major surprises, at least not of the proportions that would warrant attention from the *New York Times*. But if the human interest element is there, some newspaper will be interested, particularly if a local twist is present.

Begin by targeting a newspaper or newsletter you think would be appropriate. Clip a few recent articles from that paper on human interest stories. Analyze the content and structure of the story. Use this as your prototype. Write your story as professionally as possible, type it, and send it to the editor in charge of the appropriate department.

Another approach, particularly if you have discovered information that is more than merely readable, is to call the editorial department of a newspaper and explain who you are, what you have done, and what you have found out. Ask if the information is worthy of being written up by a reporter. You may lose the by-line this way, but if you can get yourself quoted, the benefits may be even greater. For her story about blacksmiths, Sylvia Williamson started by calling the Burlington, Vermont, *Free Press*. It ran a story that quoted Sylvia and discussed the survey. After the story appeared in the paper, she was asked to write an article for her college alumni magazine.

Finally, one more way to write up the results of a survey is to put together something similar to a press release and send it to radio stations. You might even call the news editor of a radio station and describe what you have found in your survey. You may even be invited to participate in talk shows at stations serving smaller markets.

All of this depends on what your survey results were. If you believe you have unearthed something truly startling, take the news as high up as you can. Be sure that everyone with whom you share the results knows how you did the sampling, what questions were asked, how many people you spoke with. This will clear you of any accusation about unscientific or nontechnical procedures. Your preliminary data may pique the curiosity of someone who wants to continue on with a more thorough or statistically sound study. This is actually a bonus to you as the originator of the idea and the owner of the preliminary data. However, as a zinger-seeker, you are not attempting to do a scientific study, and you need to make it clear that complex statistical results were never your goal. Some of the best and most interesting surveys were originally prompted by a small sample that yielded interesting results.

If doing a survey sounds intimidating, bring a friend along to share the work and the fun, and to take the scary edge off. You will doubtless be amazed at how open people are with a stranger and how much you will find out. Ask a question, get an answer or a hundred answers, and you might very well have a potential zinger on your hands.

Chapter 11

Work-Play:
Turning Hobbies into Achievements

Hobbies are what we do for recreation, for our own enjoyment, for the sheer interest we have in them. Zingers happen when we take hobbies one step farther.

For instance, stamp collecting, gardening, playing musical instruments, and reading novels in French are themselves interesting and enjoyable. They become zingers only when they go the next step. Writing a column on philately for the local paper, planting a garden of rare herbs and writing about it, playing a banjo you have built yourself (especially if you also compose the music), and reading novels in French and transforming them into stories to be used by high school French classes—these are all zingers. People who create such achievements make zingers out of things they like to do most.

Hobbies, which are often simple and common experiences, can grow into zingers in several ways. For instance, you may decide to share a hobby with others by writing or talking about it. The stamp collector and the gardener described above did that. Or, you may take an old hobby and give it a new twist, as the musician and the reader of French novels did.

TAKING THAT EXTRA STEP

Kevin McDermott had been a bicycle rider for years and had discovered that, as he became more adventurous about his routes, he was hard put to find good maps of out-of-the-way roads. He decided to design his own guides for cyclists and found they were interesting as well to friends and acquaintances who were hikers, cross-country skiers, and trail riders. His zinger was discovered by a small Vermont press, which hired Kevin to create a line of trail booklets.

Another person who turned his love for a common sport into an uncommon zinger—not to mention a small business—was Don Kelsey. Office-bound all winter, Don waited out the cold months until summer, when he could use his windsurfer. When he was a child, he had spent summers hanging around a boat yard near his parents' vacation home, and by the time he was grown he could manage anything that had a sail. Instead of sailing bigger boats, at which he was expert, he preferred the athletic aspects of windsurfing, which provided a terrific workout and a fast-moving skim across the water.

Noticing that kids liked to be around the boat yard just as he once had, he took an interest in teaching children to windsurf— thinking back to the time when he had looked for older kids to sail with. He found that the standard sail was much too big, and no kid-size sails were commercially available. So he cut down a large sail, made a smaller rig and mast to fit, and began giving lessons to 8- to 12-year-olds in the summer. He had taken his favorite hobby, sailing, refined it to windsurfing, and gone beyond to become entrepreneur, designer, and teacher. His resume read:

> SMALL BUSINESS: Owner "Small Sailors," Madison, Wisconsin.
>
> Started windsurfing school for children 8 to 12 years old. Designed and stitched small sail, rig, and mast for windsurfer and gave lessons to 20 students over two-month period.

Don's business expertise was in marketing in the food industry, and although this zinger did not seem to have a bearing on what he did for a living he was picked from a group of 38 applicants to interview for a vice presidency of marketing in a sporting goods company. The interviewers were easily persuaded that the skills he brought to the marketing department were crucial, but they liked most of all the fact that when he was given a choice about using his time, he used it in an imaginative way.

Whether your hobby is windsurfing or painting on fabric, sharing it with others is a sure way of turning it into a zinger. Ellen Cohen might have been content to do her batik artwork at home. However, she took her hobby public to become the mainstay of a local senior center. After exhibiting her work at the senior center, along with other local artisans, Ellen was asked to teach a weekly class. Before she knew it, she found herself swamped with holiday orders from relatives of the people in her class. She had business cards printed with a sample of one of her favorite prints and continued her zinger, which became a full-time profit-making job.

In addition to senior centers, there are many other places in

your community where you can display the fruits of your labor—
or, in the case of hobbies, your relaxation. Train and bus stations,
municipal buildings, and libraries always welcome interesting dis-
plays. Collectors take note: Ted Marcus, director of a major news-
magazine's private corporate library, is an avid collector of snow
domes, the paperweights that snow when you shake them. He arranged to display his growing collection of snow domes in the library's window during Christmastime, with a hand-lettered sign
saying, "Snow storms courtesy of Ted Marcus." Three days after
his display was up, Ted received a call from Hannah Brandberg,
another collector who was thrilled to find someone who shared her
unusual passion. They agreed to meet for dinner, and it was there
that Hannah approached Ted with the idea of doing a coffee-table
book on snow domes. Hannah eventually dropped out of the project, but Ted has gone full steam ahead and is writing and producing
the book himself, which he plans to sell to a publisher. Ted still
works full time at the library, but his book project has given him a
new focus in his life, not to mention his travels—he often manages
to arrange his trips around interviews with other collectors. After 21
years as a librarian, Ted could well be cataloguing his own books
in the near future.

Bringing your hobby to an unlikely setting is another formula
for creating successful hobbies-turned-zingers. Hence, the advice in
Chapter 6 on teaching-related zingers holds true for hobbies as well.
Sometimes it is not so much the subjects you teach or the hobby
you enjoy that makes it a zinger, but *where* you do it. This was surely
true for Bill Jellico, a gardener who not only grew flowers throughout the year in a northern climate but never tired of using them in
new ways. Bill's desk in a downtown Chicago office building had a
new plant display on it weekly. For special events like retirements,
bridal showers, or baby showers, his co-workers counted on Bill for
the floral tribute, which was always imaginative and usually donated
from his current stock of growing things, and also personalized with
some memento of meaning to the recipient.

So talented and generous was Bill with his on-site gardening
gifts that the word spread through the company. Before the second
year of Bill's employment, he formed the Tuesday Club to discuss
garden problems, office plant care, and, finally, arranging.

Unaware that he had a zinger in his life, Bill thought only that flowers and gardening were his hobby, as indeed they were. But when promotion time came around, Bill's performance was as his supervisors had hoped, with the exception of his very visible extra-curricular contributions. In a time of budget squeezing, Bill was given the highest percentage increase in the company and was told that his contributions to employee morale were greater than anyone could reasonably expect. Bill's zinger paid off, but his story is not over yet—he's considering running a green thumb consulting business from home.

What about hobbies that start out as pure fun, but then get enlarged and become commercially successful? How far a profit-making hobby can go once it takes off is the subject of another book. However, taking your hobby that second step—from sharing it with others to turning a profit on it—is a valid way to ease into a new career and revitalize your life. Unlike the short-term entrepreneurs we talked about in Chapter 5, who seized upon market gaps and filled them, our hobbyists/entrepreneurs are often surprised by the fact that something they've been enjoying their whole life is a marketable skill or commodity. And, rather than drop their businesses once they have used them for their zinger potential, hobbyists/entrepreneurs are more likely to enter into long-term business endeavors (which may come to their aid as zingers years later, as you will discover in the next chapter, "Mining Your Past for Zingers"). In any event, to inspire you to wake up to the profit potential of your own hobbies, here are some real-life stories of others who have done just that.

Eric Hunt first became enchanted by the hollow melodic sounds of steel-drum bands when he sailed to the West Indies as captain of a large educational sailing vessel used to teach marine biology and seamanship. He soon enjoyed making the music himself, which he learned from the men and boys he met on docks and in restaurants. When he had gained enough skill on the drums, he thought his new interest might please others as well. He formed a steel-drum band that plays regularly at schools, colleges, and entertainment events in the Northeast. His occupation as a sailing captain is itself a story many people want to hear. But Eric has proved himself an enterprising man, and when he someday goes after the land-based job he has in mind he will have a zinger to sell others on his entrepreneurial skill.

An age-old problem started Gail and Frank Starmer on a hobby that zinged itself into a part-time and home-based business. As Christmas Eve approached, they found themselves without gifts for numerous relatives, especially children. These Peace Corps volunteers had met in Africa and married the year after returning to the United States. They brought from their Peace Corps years a wealth of experiences, which they translated into teaching jobs, and as this holiday season approached they thought of another holiday when they had shared games with African children.

Ta-ka-radi had been the name of the game they had first seen played by children during their years of work in Africa. They asked more than once to join the games, were welcomed, and several years later they remembered the pleasure, fun, and suspense from this simple but ever-changing game.

Fifty small, wooden rectangular tiles are used to build a 17-story tower, and players are encouraged to build the tower ever higher, using only the original tiles and ingenuity. The game can quickly become hilarious—and addictive. All ages can play, although a reasonably steady hand is needed. *Ta-ka-radi* became the Starmer family's hobby, to be shared with friends, friends' children, and then, by popular request, with the world. The Starmers' idea, when they built their first sets of *Ta-ka-radi* blocks and put them in hand-sewn calico bags, was to provide original, inexpensive, and enjoyable Christmas gifts. This they surely did, but Gail is now full-time manager of the family toy business (their zinger), while Frank continues to teach and helps Gail after hours.

IMAGINATION IS THE KEY

What if your hobby is not as exotic as playing steel drums or making unusual gifts? Perhaps it is something as simple as cooking and sewing, or even watching sports on TV. It may be hard to think about marketable zingers resulting from watching pro football or baseball, but with a little imagination you might take your fascination with the local team that crucial step and make it pay. We know of a business book editor who did just that. An avid New York Mets fan, Carl Meadows kept meticulous statistics and notes on every Mets game during their championship 1986 season. He then put them together into a fun and informative booklet, which he advertised in the classifieds of various sports and baseball publications. His zinger netted him a small profit, but more importantly it enabled him to make the move from the business book arena to the sports book area, which was where his real interests lay. Even if your not-for-profit hobby is for pure relaxation, you can always turn it into a profit-making venture.

No one needed after-work relaxation more than Tracy Morgan. A teacher's aide for autistic children at a state school, Tracy always came home from work tired and frustrated by the draining work for children whose needs seemed endless to her. Yet, somehow she always found the energy and spirit to cook herself nourishing and imaginative dinners. What was pure drudgery for others was a relaxing hobby for her, one that she had enjoyed since she first learned to boil an egg. With a day crammed with demands from the children and staff at the state school, she craved independence, autonomy, and a quiet environment where the results of her work were immediately known. It was when she began to let others share the results of her at-home hobby that her zinger emerged.

She could not foresee the career that lay ahead of her, though, when a friend for whom she had made a special dessert as a gift had asked her to make another. The friend did a lot of entertaining for her husband's co-workers, and she was not an avid cook. These factors, combined with her full-time job, made her Tracy's most enthusiastic customer. After a few months of providing whole meals for her friend (and charging her for costs, plus a small amount extra for her time) Tracy realized that she had a marketable product and skill, and just for fun she put two small ads in newspapers. It was the beginning of the end of Tracy's special education career and the start of earning a living by using her cooking skills.

Tracy now works for several families five or more days a week. She plans menus, shops, cooks, and leaves meals with complete instructions for preparation. She knows people's allergies, food preferences, tastes, and needs for different kinds of events. She charges a high hourly rate, which her customers are glad to pay for the delicious high-quality meals she provides. The bachelors she works for receive "bachelor bags," single servings of varied meals, and although she counts few single women among her dozens of customers, she feels the work is wide open for expansion.

Sometimes, it is not so much our hobby that sparks a zinger, but the accommodations we make in order to enjoy it. Take the case of an inner-city artist who needs to carve out studio space within his tiny studio apartment. He might become enough of an expert on designing his own compact studio that he can build a zinger from *this* expertise, and not from his creations alone. Then there is the quintessential case of the writer who wrestles with writer's block and eventually ends up doing an article or book on how she overcame it. If you not only look at *what* you do for enjoyment, but also at *how* you do it, you may come up with some ways to turn the act of solving a problem itself into an achievement.

For Valerie Hoskins Stewart, it was the changes she made to enjoy her hobby that led not only to a business venture, but a viable zinger as well. You could say that Valerie's hobby was her children. She was holding down a full-time job in a Saint Paul, Minnesota, insurance company when she realized that she envied her babysitter. After she and her husband had their fourth child she could not face the daily hassles—including commuting—involved with her career. Very reluctantly, she gave up the promise of advancement in her field to stay home. She immediately realized that although she had envied her babysitter, one important factor was missing in her life with children—other adults. Like many a working person who thinks he or she wants to work at home, she found the lack of stimulation from co-workers to be a great loss.

Valerie's answer to the longing for adults was to turn her home into Greenhouse, a bed-and-breakfast near the city. Valerie's spacious house was too large even for four growing children, as it had been built long ago for a family with household help. So two spare bedrooms became guest bedrooms, and Valerie specialized in offering guest space to families with children who came as visitors to area hospitals.

Now that Valerie's children are grown with children of their own, she has made overtures to her old employer and other insurance companies in the Saint Paul area. Her zinger has attracted interest, and it has also helped her explain to interviewers why she dropped out of the insurance business. Her description of marketing, managing, and profiting from her zinger is an impressive recitation. At the same time, she is also considering the offer of a major hotel chain to join its management training program with the promise of accelerated promotion possibilities because of her experience. Time will tell which way her zinger takes her.

HOW TO TURN ENJOYMENT
INTO ACHIEVEMENT

As you can tell from the stories of people in this chapter, there is no one right way to turn the enjoyment you get from your hobby into an achievement you can put on your resume or use in a job interview—or even make money on. The common denominator is that these people all took their own real interests and went a step beyond ordinary participation. To start thinking about how you can do this with your hobby, ask yourself the brainstorming questions in the exercise that follows.

* * * *

Exercise: Bridging the Gap Between Hobby and Zinger

1. What sets me apart from others who also enjoy the same hobby, and how would I make that known on a resume or in a job interview?
2. How can I make my hobby accessible to those who wouldn't normally participate in it—the handicapped, children, hospital patients, for instance?
3. Where can I display the results of my hobby in my commu-

nity? At the library, schools, municipal buildings, train or bus stations?

4. How can I get the word out about my hobby? In the local paper? The company newsletter?
5. How can I share my hobby with people at work?
6. Who might be interested in paying for my creations, and how can I reach those people?
7. What special conditions does my hobby require that might in themselves be zinger material?
8. Do I use a company's product in an unusual way when participating in my hobby, and if so how could I let the company know and possibly get some PR?
9. How can I take a passive hobby—like going to the ballet or theater or watching spectator sports—and demonstrate my expertise to others?
10. Can any of my favorite hobbies be taken a step further by using the methods from previous chapters?

* * * *

Remember, for brainstorming to really work you have to refrain from making any judgments until after you have finished. No matter how wild your ideas sound, write them down. Review them later to see if they are possible. Chances are you will discover a wellspring of untapped creativity and a hobby-turned-zinger in the making.

Chapter 12

Pick and Shovel:
Mining Your Past for Zingers

Sometimes zingers are needed in a hurry. There is no time to think up an idea and execute it, yet you find yourself in a situation where your history sounds drab for the occasion. Perhaps you have decided to apply for a job for which you are qualified, but that will bring dozens of other well-qualified candidates out of the woodwork. You had not expected a position such as this one to come along, but here it is—and you want it. This is the time to mine your past for zingers.

Most people have experiences and successes in the past that can be dusted off and used when needed. Opportunities that might ultimately be zingers can be stored up so that a reservoir of achievements is always ready. Because most zingers require planning, foresight, and energy, it is wise to anticipate both the zinger and its potential use. Consider the following group of people, none of whom had set forth to create zingers, but all of whom knew that these were what they had on their hands when they were later asked to elaborate on certain achievements.

Twenty-six years after graduation from college, Claire Gallagher decided to realize a long-standing desire to go to architecture school. When it came time to fill out her application, however, she came dangerously close to putting her goal right back on the shelf. From her full-time work as a mother and part-time work in a graphics studio, Claire felt unable to pick out any singular achievements to highlight on her application. Compounding her frustration were feelings left over from college days that no one had taken her seriously because she had devoted so much energy to socializing and sorority functions. When discussing the matter with her husband, however, he reminded Claire about a recent achievement, one she was ready to dismiss as yet more evidence of her tendency to be the social butterfly.

Claire had volunteered to head the organization of her college graduating class's 25th reunion, an event that included three full days of activities and speakers. She ended up bringing back to Burlington, Vermont more members of the class and raising more money than had been done for any previous class in the past 18 years. She persuaded the classmate who had become the most famous (by publishing a wildly popular best-seller) to come back and deliver the opening address and then take the lead part in a clever skit about the class, then and now. By the end of the reunion weekend, there was no doubt in anyone's mind that Claire had a lot more going for her than her ability to party. And, with the reunion victory behind her, Claire had taken on the position of fiscal agent, the chief fund raiser for her class.

By seeing this activity in a new light, Claire was able to mine her past for other social activities that were, indeed, achievements and complete her application with confidence. At the moment she is doing beautifully as a second-year student who will no doubt become a successful architect.

May Stapleton, a young lawyer, put together a "What's Out, What's In" list for a newspaper in Memphis one year just for a lark, and was asked to do it on a semi-annual basis. It was quick, it was clever, and it got her noticed in the community. May's collection of what was and wasn't trendy had great appeal for the crowd to which she was directing her marketing efforts. It also appealed to the partners at the law firm where she worked, who were delighted as clients relayed positive reactions about May's feature. One client who called wanting May to represent him in a suit against his former employer said, "It was clear to me from the 'What's Out, What's In' list that May was clever—the kind of person I needed in order to win this suit." Once May realized that something she had thought of as merely *fun* was a drawing card for prospective clients, she decided to display her features in her office, along with her degrees and bar certification, and even wrote some other features on local trends as well.

Percy Yates was working in his family's wholesale fruit company in Georgia when he took on the task of writing a business plan for a struggling artist, an old friend from college who had creative talents to spare but little understanding of how to generate revenues from his custom-made line of stationery products. When the plan was delivered, along with help on how to begin implementation, Percy decided some of the farms that the fruit distributorship did business with could be helped by a similar experience. By offering his expertise in this area to two farms, he increased business in both firms, which pleased his father. The final result was a nice promotion for Percy at the end of the year.

Years later, this zinger was to come in handy again. When Percy wanted to move from the small, family-run operation to a larger company, he had to counter an old assumption: that he had reached his position not because of his achievements, but because of his family ties. To turn interview situations in his favor, he mined his past for zingers and came up with the business plans he developed for his artist friend and for the two farms. By citing the bottom-line results of his planning help, he was able to overcome the interviewers' skepticism, and eventually he was hired by a large firm.

Megan Burke mined her past to come up with just the zinger she needed to create the opportunity for which she was looking. A nurse for more than 20 years, Megan was more than burned out. For seven years she had been taking courses in a part-time MBA program in Boulder, Colorado, continuing her nursing career and planning for the future. As she neared the end, the idea of starting her own business (a store-front medical facility for children only) began to appeal to her more and more. With a partner, another health professional enrolled in her MBA program, she began to make the rounds of banks and financial institutions to look for backing. The two were turned down at one lending establishment after another, even though they had a sound business plan and were highly competent. Their lack of expertise in the business world kept doing them in.

Finally, the pair decided to go to a venture capitalist. They knew their return on investment would be less, but their goal was as much to realize what had now become a dream as to make a million bucks.

Megan searched her past for proof that she could in fact accomplish the task she and her partner had decided upon: owning and operating a series of store-front emergency rooms that catered exclusively to the pediatric crowd. She needed something beyond the well-prepared business plan to take to financiers in order to prove she had the stamina, the drive, the energy, ambition, and resourcefulness to make her dream happen.

Over a glass of wine one evening with Carolyn, an old friend from her early days in the pediatric ward of a major Colorado hospital, she remembered the zinger she needed. Seven years earlier the two had discovered that many parents whose children were patients in their ward asked about help for a recovering child when that child returned home from the hospital. Feeling anxious about the kind of attention kids with complex recovery patterns needed, parents often consulted the ward nurses to solicit names of free-lance health-care workers to help them out. Knowing how mothers of newborns were helped in a similar situation through a service established by an outside agency, Megan and Carolyn decided to launch a similar venture. They put together a roster of names and phone numbers, carefully checked out each person's references, and had the list printed and made available to interested parents. Throughout the next two years, the two women stayed on top of this referral service by screening new medical personnel who wanted to be put on the list, marketing the service to other hospitals, and eventually turning it into a profitable business by charging the free-lancers for each referral that evolved into an actual assignment. After another year, they sold the service for a modest sum to another nurse, but the experience was the zinger Megan needed to persuade a financial backer she was a good risk.

Searching through your past may be fruitful in unearthing some activities that could act as zingers now or be taken a step further, as Megan Burke did, to create a mega-zinger. A stack of resumes from professional people who have applied for middle- to senior-level management positions reveals zingers. Tucked away under categories called "Additional Information," "Personal," "Activities and Interests," or "Special Triumphs" are the following golden nuggets:

1. Wrote musical for community theater group and helped produce show.
2. Champion ski jumper for seven seasons.
3. Certified SCUBA instructor.
4. Designed and built an igloo to house 12 people for one month as part of an experiment in winter camping. Prepared all food, slept, dressed, and lived in the ice building.
5. Speak Farsi (Iranian) fluently.
6. Researched and wrote booklet on Shelter Island, New York. Designed and led VIP tours of the island.
7. Illustrated several pages of a textbook on birds.
8. Built a sugar house; make maple syrup each spring, encouraging school groups to tour and help with production.

9. Brown Belt in Kung-Fu.
10. Stenciled rooms in several friends' houses.
11. Restored a 1687 house for town's bicentennial celebration.
12. Acted as subject and informant for *National Geographic Magazine*'s study of one-room schoolhouses.
13. Runway model for nationally known modeling agency.
14. Designed a money belt/passport pouch and marketed it to sporting goods manufacturer.
15. Wrote travel features for the *Washington Post*.

A useful exercise is to create a mega-zinger for each of the foregoing activities, to take them all a bit farther and make more of them. Collecting a group to brainstorm aloud will make the task go quickly and well.

Employment recruiters who make actual hiring and promotion decisions responded to these zingers by answering the following question: Why might you be attracted to the person who possesses this zinger, assuming other factors such as skills, experience, and personality are appropriate? Here are their answers, corresponding to each of the previously listed achievements:

1. This is obviously a creative, high-energy, and talented individual.
2. I would assume this person is not afraid of taking risks. Sounds like a bold and daring personality.
3. This person has worked hard for the credential. I know; I tried to get a SCUBA certificate at one time in my life and never pulled it off.
4. I would be intrigued by someone who would build and live in an ice house for a month. I would want to hear all about the experience and I would guess that this person has a wonderful spirit of adventure.
5. If this person is not Iranian, I would be interested in how he learned the language and why. This skill would not fit into my business, but it is a difficult language so I would want to know more about the person who learned it.
6. Here is a person who is passionate about a geographic spot.

I like that extent of interest in a place, an activity, anything.

7. I would want to see the book; if the pictures were of professional quality, I would be impressed. Sounds like real talent.
8. I know how much work is involved with this one so I have immediate respect for anyone who does sugaring.
9. Impressive. A distinct honor earned by hard work and tenacity.
10. Does this person have pictures? Did the job look like it was professionally done? I am interested in knowing more.
11. Here is another one that makes one want to ask lots of questions. Did the person do the job by himself? Where did he learn the skills? Unless this guy is a carpenter by trade, I would be impressed by the accomplishment.
12. I am very impressed by anyone who gets a magazine of that caliber to come and interview her.
13. When we were told this woman graduated from an Ivy League university with honor grades we were interested. We were intrigued by her combination of talents and abilities.
14. This sounds like a creative and ambitious person. I would want to see a sample and find out if it is selling well and if the person made any money from the product.
15. How did he or she get this assignment? This person must either be a terrific writer or have had some very interesting experiences on the road.

These responses echo much of what we have talked about in this book. Zingers attract attention, draw people to you, represent creativity and leadership. They take you one step closer to getting whatever it is you want.

This book has illustrated a wide variety of people and achievements in order to show the range of situations, circumstances, and arenas for using the zinger. It also demonstrates that opportunities for creating zingers are endless. To lead a zinger-filled life, keep your eyes and ears open, constantly be alert to possibilities, take some risks, and be receptive to new ideas. Good luck as you go out zinger hunting. The woods are filled with possible achievements, and you can zing them home.

Index

About the Authors

Dr. Joanna Henderson is currently Director of Graduate Admissions at Babson College in Wellesley, Massachusetts. She was formerly a marketing manager and Director of Professional Recruitment at McGraw-Hill. Dr. Henderson and co-author Betty Lou Marple each contributed a chapter to *Not as Far as You Think,* a Lexington Book.

Dr. Betty Lou Marple is currently Assistant Dean at the Harvard University Graduate School of Design, where she manages the Office of Special Programs. In her 30 years in the field of Higher Education Adminstration, she has run continuing education and other programs as well as counseled students on careers and related matters at Wellesley College, Brandeis University, and Radcliffe College.